Paul Hannon

HILLSIDE

HILLSIDE GUIDES - ACROSS THE NORTH

Long Distance Walks
•COAST TO COAST WALK •CLEVELAND WAY COMPANION
•WESTMORLAND WAY •FURNESS WAY •CUMBERLAND WAY
•DALES WAY •LADY ANNE'S WAY •NORTH BOWLAND TRAVERSE

Circular Walks - Lancashire
•BOWLAND •PENDLE & THE RIBBLE

Circular Walks - Yorkshire Dales
•HOWGILL FELLS •THREE PEAKS •MALHAMDALE
•WHARFEDALE •NIDDERDALE •WENSLEYDALE •SWALEDALE

Circular Walks - North York Moors
•WESTERN MOORS •SOUTHERN MOORS •NORTHERN MOORS

Circular Walks - South Pennines
•BRONTE COUNTRY •CALDERDALE •ILKLEY MOOR

Circular Walks - Peak District
•EASTERN PEAK • NORTHERN PEAK • CENTRAL PEAK
• SOUTHERN PEAK • WESTERN PEAK

Circular Walks - North Pennines
•TEESDALE •EDEN VALLEY

Hillwalking - Lake District
•OVER LAKELAND MOUNTAINS •OVER LAKELAND FELLS

Yorkshire Pub Walks
•HARROGATE/WHARFE VALLEY •HAWORTH/AIRE VALLEY

Large format colour hardback

FREEDOM OF THE DALES

BIKING COUNTRY
•YORKSHIRE DALES CYCLE WAY •WEST YORKSHIRE CYCLE WAY
•MOUNTAIN BIKING - WEST & SOUTH YORKSHIRE
•AIRE VALLEY BIKING GUIDE •CALDERDALE BIKING GUIDE
• GLASGOW Clyde Valley & Loch Lomond

• YORK WALKS City Theme Walks

•WALKING COUNTRY TRIVIA QUIZ Over 1000 questions

Send S.A.E. for a detailed catalogue and pricelist

WALKING COUNTRY

NORTHERN PEAK

Paul Hannon

HILLSIDE

HILLSIDE
PUBLICATIONS
11 Nessfield Grove
Keighley
West Yorkshire
BD22 6NU

First published 1997

© Paul Hannon 1997

ISBN 1 870141 48 2

The author would like to acknowledge the assistance of Roland Smith, Head of Information Services at the Peak National Park, for his invaluable help in looking over the manuscript. Any errors, however, remain the author's.

Cover illustrations:
Mam Tor; Blackden Brook, Kinder; Kinder Downfall
Back cover: Seal Edge, Kinder Scout
(Paul Hannon/Big Country Picture Library)

Page 1: Edale Cross
Page 3: Plaque in Bowden Bridge Quarry, Hayfield

Printed in Great Britain by
Carnmor Print and Design
95-97 London Road
Preston
Lancashire
PR1 4BA

CONTENTS

INTRODUCTION

THE PEAK NATIONAL PARK

The Peak District was designated Britain's first National Park in 1951, and embracing an area of 555 square miles it is the most popular in the country. While commonly allotted to Derbyshire, substantial parts fall within Staffordshire, Yorkshire and Cheshire. *Peak* is in fact a misnomer, for it is plainly evident that peaks are in very short supply here: it derives from *Pecsaetan* ('hill-dweller'), tribes that occupied the area long before the Normans came.

The Peak divides into two distinctive areas, the Dark Peak and the White Peak. These refer to the principal rocks, millstone grit (gritstone) in the Dark Peak and limestone in the White Peak. The Dark Peak horseshoe encloses the limestone country, with the high moors of Kinder Scout and Bleaklow to the north and long arms reaching down either side. That in the east traces the Derwent Valley south in a series of abrupt edges: that to the west is disjointed, resurrecting itself above Buxton to run south, largely less dramatically, west of the Manifold Valley. The northern massif is typified by vast tracts of peat bog and heather, a world away from the White Peak's softer terrain.

The compact White Peak offers green dales overlooked by gleaming cliffs. Unlike the limestone country of the Yorkshire Dales, it has few potholes and pavements: its speciality is valleys, exemplified by the likes of Lathkill Dale, the river Wye and the incomparable Dovedale. Much of the White Peak is an upland plateau where old lead mining communities huddle. The area is dissected by drystone walls, and though large-scale quarrying is all too evident, farming remains the traditional source of employment, increasingly supplemented by tourism. While one railway survives to run through the heart of the Park, several others have been converted to leisure trails: they provide excellent cross-country routes linking numerous towns and villages.

Bakewell is the largest community in the National Park, but it is the small towns on the fringe, such as Buxton, Ashbourne, Matlock, Leek, Chapel en le Frith and Glossop, that act as major centres. Though this whole area might be encircled in a day's car tour, once you get out in the fresh air you will quickly appreciate the rich diversity of country that offers many happy years of real exploring - on foot.

NORTHERN PEAK

The northern reaches of the Peak District consist of a range of broad-shouldered moorland heights divided by deep valleys, around which lesser scale moorlands are scattered. The central massifs, Kinder Scout, Bleaklow and Black Hill are vast, though each is also riven by deep-sided cloughs that drive hard into the heart of the moors. With no centres of population this sparsely inhabited wild country looks to the small towns on the fringe, such as Glossop, New Mills, Chapel en le Frith and Holmfirth. Glossop itself is a good base for many of these walks, as is smaller Hayfield, nearby, though it is perhaps left to Edale to take centre stage, a popular village suitably located at the foot of Kinder Scout.

Two main valleys dissect the heights, the Woodlands Valley between Kinder and Bleaklow, and Longdendale between Bleaklow and Black Hill. Despite its notoriety - partly a result of bad Pennine Way experiences - Kinder is the least lonely, isolated or extensive of the three. To many Bleaklow is the finest, and undoubtedly the hardest to really get to know. Black Hill is lowest of the three, by a small margin, but is arguably even less explored.

To the west gentler hills overlook the Sett Valley, though the likes of Cracken Edge and Lantern Pike should disappoint no-one. To the north, the moorlands begin their inexorable march north, though for the most part their allegiance to corners of Lancashire and Yorkshire see them looked upon more as South Pennine than Peak. Southwards the Mam Tor ridge marks the transformation into gentler country of the *Central Peak*, while the Upper Derwent Valley forms the eastern limits of this book. Across it, similar heather moors decline southwards to the onset of the celebrated eastern edges, represented in the companion *Eastern Peak*.

The Northern Peak is composed of millstone grit, a dark, rounded rock that breaks the surface either in scattered boulders or more typical escarpments. Gritstone edges are found in many locations, notably on the edges of the Kinder plateau, and more disjointedly on Bleaklow, principally its northern flank. Black Hill offers its own examples, as do the lesser heights. Ground cover is for the most part miles of rolling heather interspersed with peat bogs, rough grasses, cotton grass and marsh. Bracken claims some of the steeper flanks and cloughs, with native woodland poorly represented. Most common wildife encountered is the ubiquitous red grouse, though one of the finest sights is the mountain hare, especially noble in its pure white winter garb.

Access

Just a few decades ago, the high moors of the Peak were in the front line of the struggle for our present day freedoms. Progress was successful due to the heroic campaigns of the early ramblers; being on the doorsteps of towns and cities, the accessibility of this fine playground was the catalyst for action. Access agreements negotiated by the Peak Park have opened up great tracts - around 80 square miles - of country, and subject to a few days' closure at times of shooting, and possibly at times of high fire risk, this land is very nearly ours. In addition, walkers are almost universally welcome in the large areas of countryside in the hands of the National Trust. Most of these areas are clearly marked on the 1:25,000 Outdoor Leisure map (see overleaf).

Though there are various rights of way over the moors - many followed in this book - a number of the walks take advantage of the access agreements to earn more rewarding explorations. These walks gain and depart access areas at designated entry points (marked 'Boundary of Open Country' on signs). These are by way of either public or permissive paths. References to *Open Country* in the text specifically mean Access Land, rather than open countryside generally. Please adhere to these requirements, as well as observing the other by-laws. Please also remember to obey legitimate signs encountered on your walks: rights of way can be opened, closed or diverted. On these occasions official notices take precedence over the guidebook.

It is important to remember that many of these walks cross wild, inhospitable terrain, and though the majority are on some kind of path it is nevertheless essential to carry and know how to use a compass, in conjunction with the map which should be with you as a matter of course. This applies doubly to Bleaklow and Black Hill. The Bleaklow massif is larger than Kinder, with fewer paths and people, and less easy to escape from if conditions take a turn for the worse.

Finally, please take extra care to respect the life and work of the Peak. Its very accessibility puts it in the firing line when we all want to escape into the country at the same time. If we take nothing more than photographs and leave only the slightest of footprints, then this wonderful landscape will be in good shape for the next generation. In particular, ensure that dogs are kept on leads and that you close any gates you have opened. Many of the moors are coveted as grouse shooting grounds, and as with any private property, shooting butts and cabins encountered should be respected.

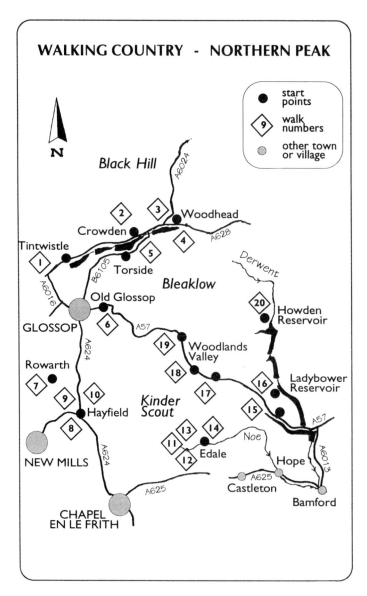

WALKING COUNTRY - NORTHERN PEAK

N

- ● start points
- ◇ 9 walk numbers
- ● other town or village

Black Hill

A6024

◇ 2   ◇ 3   Woodhead

Crowden   ◇ 4   A628

Tintwistle   ◇ 5   Derwent

◇ 1   Torside   *Bleaklow*

B6105   A6016

Old Glossop   ◇ 20   Howden Reservoir

GLOSSOP   ◇ 6   A57

A624   ◇ 19   Woodlands Valley

Rowarth   ◇ 18   Ladybower Reservoir

◇ 7   ◇ 10   ◇ 17   ◇ 16

◇ 9   *Kinder Scout*   ◇ 15   A57

Hayfield   ◇ 13   ◇ 14   A6013

◇ 8   ◇ 11   Noe

A624   ◇ 12   Edale   Hope

NEW MILLS   A625   Castleton   Bamford

CHAPEL EN LE FRITH

Getting around

One road and one railway line put most of this area within easy reach: the A57 runs through the Snake Pass in the heart of the Northern Peak from Glossop to Sheffield, while the Sheffield-Manchester (Hope Valley) railway is a direct route into the action, with particularly useful stations at Chinley, Edale, Hope and Bamford. The cul-de-sac lines to Glossop and Buxton can also be useful.

Numerous seasonal bus services operate on less regular routes such as the Snake Pass, and worthy of special mention are those serving the Upper Derwent Valley, on the edge of our area: additionally, when the road beyond Fairholmes visitor centre is closed a minibus runs to the road-end at Howden Reservoir. With a little planning, various permutations can be created by linking different sections of the walks, to create longer routes or to take advantage of public transport. Starting points with public transport, however limited, are indicated, along with other useful information, at the start of each walk.

Using the guide

Each walk is self-contained, with essential information being followed by a simple map and concise description of the route. Dovetailed between this are useful notes of features along the way, and interspersed are illustrations which both capture the flavour of the walks and record the many items of interest. In order to make the instructions easier to follow, essential route description has been highlighted in bold type, while items in lighter type refer to historical asides and things to look out for: in this format you can find your way more easily while still locating features of interest at the relevant point in the text.

The simple sketch maps identify the location of the routes rather than the fine detail, and whilst the route description should be sufficient to guide you around, an Ordnance Survey map is recommended: the route can easily be plotted on the relevant OS map. To gain the most from a walk, the detail of the 1:25,000 maps is unsurpassed. They also serve to vary walks as desired, giving an improved picture of one's surroundings and the availability of linking paths. This area is fortunate in that just one map gives complete coverage of the walks:-

• *Outdoor Leisure Sheet 1 - Peak District, Dark Peak*

Also extremely useful for general planning purposes are the Landranger maps at 1:50,000, and again, one single sheet covers the entire area:
110 - Sheffield & Huddersfield

One further planning aid is the OS Touring Map which covers the whole National Park at the scale of 1:63,360 (1 inch to the mile).

SOME USEFUL ADDRESSES

Ramblers' Association   1/5 Wandsworth Road, London SW8 2XX
Tel. 0171-582 6878

Peak National Park Office
Aldern House, Baslow Road, Bakewell DE45 1AE
Tel. 01629-814321

Edale Visitor Centre   Tel. 01433-670207

Torside Visitor Centre   On B6105 , Torside Reservoir, Longdendale
(weekends only, closed in winter)

Fairholmes Visitor Centre   Upper Derwent Valley
Tel. 01433-650953 (weekends only in winter)

Castleton Visitor Centre   Tel. 01433-620679 (weekends in winter)

Tourist Information
The Gatehouse, Victoria Street **Glossop** SK13 8HT
Tel. 01457-855920

Peak & Northern Footpaths Society
Mr E Sutton, 1 Crossfield Grove, Marple Bridge, Cheshire SK6 5EQ
Tel. 0161 427 3582

Friends of National Parks
Council for National Parks, 246 Lavender Hill, London SW11 1LJ
Tel. 0171-924 4077

Derbyshire Wildlife Trust
Elvaston Castle, Derby DE7 3ET
Tel. 01332-756610

The National Trust   High Peak Estate Office
Edale End, Edale Rd, Hope, via Sheffield S30 2RF
Tel. 01433-70368

Bus enquiries: 01246-250450;   **Train enquiries:** 0161-832 8353

ARNFIELD MOORS

START *Tintwistle*   *Grid ref. SE 022973*

DISTANCE *9½ miles*

ORDNANCE SURVEY MAPS
1:50,000
Landranger 110 - Sheffield & Huddersfield
1:25,000
Outdoor Leisure 1 - Peak District, Dark Peak

ACCESS *Start from the green in the heart of the old village. Tintwistle is served by bus from numerous Manchester area locations, largely via Glossop. Hadfield railway station is 1 mile distant (trains from Manchester via Glossop).* • *ACCESS AREA - see page 8.*

Most of the miles are moorland strides in this large circuit on the western limits of the Black Hill massif. Though the walking is generally easy, map and compass are strongly recommended.

Ⓢ Tintwistle admirably mixes its National Park status with its edge of the working world position: big factories on one side, big wild grouse moors on the other; and then, the reservoirs of Longdendale begin here. The centre is an attractive spot, focused around a war memorial on a sloping green: a white walled pub, the *Bulls Head*, a former toll house and former weavers' cottages complete the scene. The church, meanwhile stands aloof across the busy A57 that happily runs parallel to the village street, though very close: there are shops and more pubs on the main road below.

From the war memorial head along Arnfield Lane, which immediately leaves the houses behind. A very neat arrangement of setts is lost to a normal surface at a junction above Crossgates Farm. So begins a thousand feet of climbing to gain the moortop. Here are good views to the left over Arnfield Reservoir. **Running on to Arnfield avoid the temptation of a path to Open Country, and continue to the crossing of Arnfield Brook. Just up the slope, leave the road to go left into Arnfield hamlet, and turn sharp right up a steep rough track. It climbs broadly between walls to a stile into Open Country. At the junction just ahead ignore a direct shooters' track and go left with the wall-side track, running on (with a superb prospect over the moors to come) to descend to the crossing of Ogden Clough.** Here we leave the National Park for a short mile.

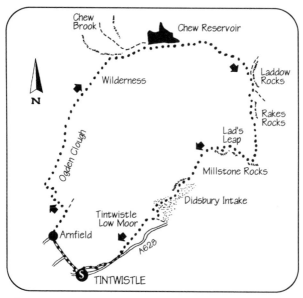

Ahead is the great sweep of Boar Flat and Arnfield Moor, and our route to the skyline heads up the slope on the opposite bank of the clough. A pleasant track climbs back to the accompanying wall, but on the brow above it cuts an angle of the wall to find a guidepost sending a slim trod off up to the right. Signposted Chew Brook, this is the way to go, a slender but always clear path graduating delightfully up the grassy slopes. It remains a gem of a route throughout its climb over Boar Flat, increasingly through heather above the steeper drop to the clough. Occasional superfluous cairns and stakes confirm its course.

Nearing the brook, a fence angle, a footbridge at a confluence and a pair of notices signify transition both of terrain and status. Cross the left arm of the brook to enter access land and the National Park for the remainder of the walk. Though no less easy, the going, beyond a cairn, enters a small patch of bracken, and as the climb becomes a little steeper stony peat based ground takes over on Ormes Moor. As the path becomes less clear, a string of cairns underline the route.

Only on the very skyline does the path completely falter as we plunge into the peaty plateau that is not labelled Wilderness for nothing. Somewhat ill-timed, the cairns falter and the sudden demise is underscored by the sight of sunken bootprints straying in all directions: it's every man for himself. Pressing straight on, the mast of Holme Moss appears to the right, and a tor on the Alphin ridge to the left: the Chew edge is not very distant! **An occasional stake may be espied to assist progress, though this wallowing in groughs is but a short interlude: a re-forming path leads through quickly improving terrain with a tiny brook on the right to a cairn/stake on the edge at Chew Hurdles.**

Its over! This spot, atop gritstone cliffs falling steeply to Chew Brook, is very much, in all respects, a place to draw breath. The brook leads the eye down to Dovestone Reservoir, with a substantial portion of the Saddleworth edges lining the sides of the clough. Ahead beyond the reservoir is the Pots & Pans obelisk above Saddleworth, with Windy Hill mast by the unseen M62 far beyond; to the right, near at hand, is the grassy embankment of Chew Reservoir. **On resuming, go right on the well defined edge path to gain the corner of Chew Reservoir.** When built in 1912, it was the highest reservoir in the country: even today, only Cow Green in Upper Teesdale can equal it.

Ignoring a water authority road descending from it, keep straight ahead on the south/near side of the dam on a broad track running its full length. At the end of the water it reduces to footpath width, quickly crossing a concrete footbridge and arriving at a confluence. A trio of cairns ease navigation, confirming that the clear path swings right with that branch. This crossing of Laddow Moss remains distinct throughout its quite short length, though the journey is a magnificent one through the heart of typical Dark Peakland.

Opposite: Laddow Rocks, looking down Crowden Great Brook to Bleaklow across Torside Reservoir

The tiny brook is crossed and re-crossed, and as it dries up a string of cairns guide the sandy path over the vague watershed. The surroundings open out somewhat to reveal wide moorscapes, with the long, dark wall of Bleaklow itself appearing far ahead to the right (and part of Kinder to its right). **The descent is even better defined, slanting right to quickly drop, improvingly on grass, to the crest of Laddow Rocks - another major halting place.**

The finest of Laddow Rocks are substantial buttresses, which played an important role in the development of rock climbing in the Peak. Here joining the Pennine Way on its ascent of Black Hill, take time to sojourn in the grass overlooking this superb prospect of the valley of Crowden Great Brook driving into the bleakest of moorland. Crowden in Longdendale is down to the right with Torside Reservoir behind.

Turning right with the descending path to Crowden, trace it for no more than a 100 or so yards. Don't go rushing headlong into the valley, unless conditions deteriorate substantially to warrant a safety move. **As the PW commences a steeper drop, take a trackless course**

to contour round the steeper 'V' of Oaken Clough. On the other side a thin path forms above the distinct edge of **Rakes Rocks**. Take your time to glimpse back at the receding prospect of Laddow from this smashing foreground.

As the rocks fade so does the path, and a second short section of open ground is faced. Without losing height head due south, noting ahead the prominent line of a collapsed wall on the near skyline. The route thereto is far gentler than might be imagined, and on approaching the top side of the wall a path rising with it is met, immediately before a well defined peat passage.

Turn right here up another such passage, waving goodbye to a final glimpse of Laddow as the path climbs to a second section of wall. Here the first of a line of cairns guides the clear path up a gentle incline, aiming for Lad's Leap on the near side of the conspicuous skyline of Millstone Rocks. At Lad's Leap, Coombes Clough is crossed and a good walk leads around the edge to Millstone Rocks.

Head off on an immediate descent (aiming for the metropolis ahead) on a quickly forming path that slants down to a fence. At the second of successive stiles leave the open moor (and Open Country) and head down a clear path through heather. Within a few yards this reveals a magnificent prospect of the final section. Below is a great tract of the colourful country of Didsbury Intake. **The mystery of where the path goes is quickly answered as a sharp corner sees it traversing along to the right beneath an imposing line of cliffs, former quarries.** This is a riotous assembly of boulders and recolonised spoil heaps, and features a ruin on the left with a stone water trough adjacent. **Towards the end it becomes a broader track.** Stone drainage channels confirm its former importance. **It angles down through scattered woodland to emerge from the intake and wind down towards the main road.**

At the wall however, double back right onto a nicer green track, which runs along to quickly becomes enclosed, continuing between walls to pass Townhead Farm and debouch onto the busy A57. Fortunately a footway is provided on our side, though within two minutes escape by a back lane (Old Road) which runs on through Tintwistle and back to the village green. En route we have a view of Bottoms Reservoir below, and pass a former Ebenezer Chapel erected for the Wesleyan Methodists in 1830.

2

LADDOW ROCKS

START *Crowden*   *Grid ref. SK 072992*

DISTANCE *6 miles*

ORDNANCE SURVEY MAPS
1:50,000
Landranger 110 - Sheffield & Huddersfield
1:25,000
Outdoor Leisure 1 - Peak District, Dark Peak

ACCESS *Start from the National Park car park on the A624. Served by Manchester-Sheffield express buses.* • *ACCESS AREA - see page 8.*

An exploration of two side valleys penetrating Black Hill. Mostly easy walking, half on the Pennine Way, half well off the beaten track.

S Crowden was once a busy little community with shops and pubs. From 1860 to 1957 it had its own railway station on the south side of the dale. Crowden Hall dated from 1692 but was demolished in 1937 by Manchester Waterworks: the campsite now occupies the site. Terraced cottages known as the Long Row were taken over as a youth hostel in 1964, serving the first stopping point on the Pennine Way's great march north. The tiny church, old vicarage and old school are just along the road east. St. James' church (Woodhead Chapel) sits on a knoll overlooking Torside Reservoir, buried here are those killed by accident or disease whilst working on the nearby railway tunnels.

From the bottom of the car park a path runs to the toilets. Turn right up the narrow lane here past the campsite to a junction. Ahead is an outdoor centre: our way goes left. This is the old road, long by-passed by the modern highway just downstream. **Continue on over the bridge and up the other side as a rough track. At the top, just short of a plantation, the PW is directed up to the right.**

Follow this grassy branch through several fields to an Open Country sign at a stile and plantation. Opposite are the slagheaps of Loftend Quarry above Crowden. Looking back, the northern edges of Bleaklow feature the Rollick Stones and Wildboar Clough. **The path runs on, remaining level for a considerable time as it undulates through the colourful country of Crowden Great Brook.** Above are increasingly rocky walls, while visible up the clough are the Castles, to which we shall attain. **Crossing a side stream the path rises to a bouldery knoll, and can be seen ahead as it runs on to climb towards Laddow Rocks.**

After crossing Oakenclough Brook (a branch contours right to pass beneath the crags) the path climbs on a recently stone pitched surface. A cairn indicates a branch left to the Chew Valley, but our obvious way remains on the edge. This rapidly forms as a delightfully thin path forges on the crest of Laddow Rocks.

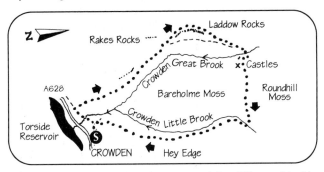

The finest moments are enjoyed as we tread the clifftops of Laddow. The best of these are substantial buttresses which played an important role in the development of rock climbing in the Peak. This is also the walk's summit. **As the crags abate the path meanders along a gentler grassy edge.** The twin nabs of Castles are close by across the brook, while ahead are Black Hill's rolling heights. **The path slants nearer the brook: at the path's lowest point, where the path from beneath the crags merges, leave it and drop down to cross the brook.**

Slant back up the steep bank to easier ground, and just to the right a stony corner is reached. Contour further right on sheeptrods to arrive at the twin prows of Castles. The first offers some shapely rocks and a superb, seldom seen view down Crowden Great Brook. **Cross to the equally inviting second, then leave by heading east, down to**

a saddle and up the slope behind. **Within minutes the moortop is gained. This 'seven minute crossing' of Roundhill Moss soon reveals the twin valley of Crowden Little Brook ahead.** As the slope forms the full scale of the valley is seen beneath Westend Moss opposite, and the increasing slopes leading up towards Black Hill. Running parallel just above the brook is the path that will return us to the start.

The easiest way bears left, slanting down, possibly crossing Wiggin Clough and ideally aiming for an attractive little waterfall. This is a fine place to linger before crossing just upstream. If Crowden Great Brook was crossable then this should be easy. Just upstream are the remains of a sheepfold. **Rise to the path and turn downstream, this same way leading almost all the way back. Initially a superb old shooters' path, it contours round to the head of a modern bulldozed track. Forge on as it runs down the valley, virtually level all the way.**

Beneath the spoil heaps of Loftend Quarry we quit Open Country and the track drops down. As it curves around beneath the spoil, descend to a stile in the fence below, from where a clear path continues down the steeper slope.

Crowden is almost beneath our feet now. At a lower stile a cobbled track is met on a bend. Go down this to a ladder-stile, and with the outdoor centre just ahead, go left on a path to join its drive out onto the junction by the campsite, with the start just ahead.

Waterfall,
Crowden Little Brook

3

BLACK HILL

START *Woodhead*   *Grid ref. SE 098007*

DISTANCE *7½ miles*

ORDNANCE SURVEY MAPS
1:50,000
Landranger 110 - Sheffield & Huddersfield
1:25,000
Outdoor Leisure 1 - Peak District, Dark Peak

ACCESS *Start from Heyden Bridge on the A6024 up to Holme Moss. Unfortunately the abandoned section of road to the old bridge is padlocked, but there is a lay-by opposite and ample verge parking. An eccentric alternative is to start from the car park on the Yorkshire side of Holme Moss summit. Though little short of the walk's highest point, in practice it works quite well. Served by Summer Sunday/BH Monday Huddersfield-Glossop buses. • ACCESS AREA - see page 8.*

Rough and pathless for much of the way, this is not the easiest of walks. But the surroundings are wild and grand, you'll see few other folk, and there's no denying Black Hill has a certain majesty. Black Hill is also the highest point of traditional Cheshire, a fact overlooked by many since local government reorganisation in 1974. Before commencing, note the sight of Holme Moss's great transmitter mast on the skyline ahead: in time we'll be walking past that! Map and compass are strongly recommended.

❺ **From the locked gate walk back a few yards towards Woodhead then go up the bank to a stile into the trees (not quite as per map). Here a footpath to Open Country begins, quickly rising to a quarry and becoming at once indistinct. In the quarry bowl clamber up left and resume on a part-sunken way up through a well-defined gap in the trees. This winds up, at times roughly, to a stile onto open moor.**

The sunken way resumes, slanting gently left across otherwise rough terrain. Down to the left heavy waggons rumble over the bridge on Woodhead Reservoir. **As the going eases the old track loses its way. With the side valley of Oaksike Clough to the left, rise up to easier ground on the grassier edge just above.** Far up to the right is the upper reach of the Holme Moss mast.

Bear left along the edge to approach the head of the clough. The sheeptrod we have been tracing forks after a tiny side-stream, and though either way will do, a better aligned trod branches up to the right, keeping above the stream. With luck this faint way leads unerringly up, with a rough grassy plateau in front and the better defined knoll of Westend Moss ahead.

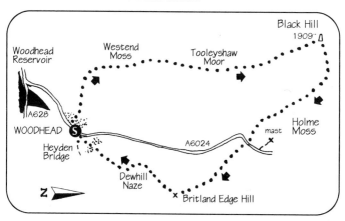

Simply rise straight up the grassy way between rougher ground, a very easy walk closing in on the brook as we approach the base of the knoll. Just over to the left, on the slope, are the remains of a small sheepfold marked on the map. Continue up Stonefold Grough to emerge onto the peaty edge of the plateau. Forge straight on, with the mast revealed ahead. The beginnings of the stream can be traced a short way up through the grough walls before climbing out to better discern the lie of the land.

The mast is almost fully in view now straight ahead, not looking very distant at all. Don't make a bee-line for it but bear left, north-west, possibly passing a sizeable pool before merging into the public

footpath on White Low, marked by several stakes up to this point. Black Hill is outspread ahead now, and views increase to the west. The return route is also in clearer view over to the right across the deep valley of Heyden Brook used by the road.

Bear right along this clear path, rising ever gently over Tooleyshaw Moor. The walking alternates from level, part moist sections of grass to pleasant, steeper peaty moments. Looking back down past Bleaklow's western arm is a section of Kinder Scout. **For the most part this is easy and enjoyable walking, often on stony ways between groughs to emerge on the flatter top of Tooleyshaw Moss. Here the groughs part like the Red Sea and a more eerie landscape, nevertheless still easy, sees us across the penultimate stage.**

Fairly frequent cairns serve us from this point. The final stage is unmistakable: this is what Black Hill promised and has not failed to deliver. Note that looking back, we are now heading almost directly away from the mast. At a fence-stile the hill lives up to its name for the last stage, as with the Ordnance Survey column in view a black, peaty route must be sought to grasp the trig point at 1909ft/582m.

A further challenge to gaining OS column 2958 is its several feet of foundations around which the peat has long eroded away! In the worst conditions - especially for the solitary rambler - it may be wise to omit this final stage, for the slutchy depths may otherwise ensure it is your very FINAL stage! Not surprisingly the view is rather lacklustre, the girth of the summit plateau permitting little of interest to reveal itself. The name Soldier's Lump is also appended to Black Hill's summit, in deference to the Royal Engineers who erected one of the earliest triangulation stations here in 1784.

Leave with caution, bound for the road summit beyond the mast, though a bee-line is once again not the way. Instead, aiming left of the mast, bear east across ground easier, at least, than those final minutes to the top. Fairly quickly things open out. Meeting the earlier fence, go left to its corner where it crosses the head of Heyden Brook. Here the fence turns sharp right to run above the clough, and a clear path does likewise.

The path shadows the fence then contours straight on as the fence drops away. An intervening stile in a cross-fence is met and the way resumes very pleasantly and easily with stone's throw fences above

and below. Even at occasional fainter moments there are no doubts, as the object of tracing the well-defined edge of the peat margin remains the same. Further, just past the mast, another fence is met. From the stile here bear left over gentle peat ground to join the road.

It is worth detouring two minutes along to the left to enjoy the motorists' view over the Holme Valley, with Yateholme Reservoir and surrounding plantations below, and Holmfirth down the valley. If the BBC mast often appears shrouded in cloud, that is because it reaches an incredible 750ft into the sky!

If you landed on the road at the right spot, cross to the Derbyshire sign and a stile back onto the moor. Access land to our right is defined by a fence heading south-east away from the road. A thin path shadows it and generally easy going leads on through an intervening fence. Ahead, Bleaklow increasingly dominates; looking back, Laddow Rocks slot neatly in the saddle beneath Tooleyshaw Moor.

The watershed fence takes us down to a minor peaty saddle then up the other side to a pronounced bend on the crest of Britland Edge Hill (1719ft/524m). Though a trod remains with the fence, we leave it and advance no more than fifty yards right to find a well defined edge and a few stones. Down below is a plateau with another minor edge beyond it (and Woodhead Reservoir in the valley). Drop down, bearing to the right end of this edge. Down below is a long stretch of the road as it climbs to the mast. **Bear left along this peaty edge, easiest going being along its foot until a stony scarp takes shape.**

Two minutes along the top of this brings arrival at the sharp nab of Dewhill Naze. At this point we leave it, first getting bearings by locating the right side of the top of a plantation across the plateau below. Descend by an old wall then cross to follow another old wall on the left, aiming for the reservoir. At the end by the plantation drop quickly to the bottom corner, now between plantations. Take a gate in the left corner and through the crumbling wall bend. The road is immediately below now, and the start point is only minutes away.

Take an old pathway down the wall-side on the left, and towards the end cross to a gateway in the wall below. Drop down the field to join a track at the bottom, and turn right on it to a stile and gate, out of Open Country and onto the road. The start is just down to the left.

4

BLEAKLOW STONES

START *Woodhead*   *Grid ref. SK 114998*

DISTANCE *8 miles*

ORDNANCE SURVEY MAPS
1:50,000
Landranger 110 - Sheffield & Huddersfield
1:25,000
Outdoor Leisure 1 - Peak District, Dark Peak

ACCESS *Start from the entrance to the Woodhead Tunnel on the A628 at the head of Longdendale. There is a car park on the road above, and car parking to the south of the road on the cul-de-sac road to the tunnel entrances. Served by Summer Sunday/BH Monday Sheffield-Glossop buses. • ACCESS AREA - see page 8.*

A splendid approach to the wild heights of Bleaklow, followed by a typical moorland skyline walk and concluding surprisingly quickly and easily. Map and compass strongly recommended.

S The Woodhead Tunnel burrows for three miles beneath the Pennine watershed, created to carry the Manchester-Sheffield railway via the Etherow and Don valleys. Opened in 1845, a second tunnel followed 7 years later, and as recently as 1954 a third, far bigger replacement was completed. Its lifespan was short, however, as the line closed in 1981, 11 years after passenger services ceased. West of the tunnel, the line has been converted into the Longdendale Trail, a seven mile route ideal for cyclists and equestrians (see WALK 5).

Cross the bridge and turn sharp left over a stile. A broad track runs upstream with the river Etherow. Here little more than a moorland brook, the Etherow once flowed happily for many a mile through Longdendale before being largely displaced by a string of reservoirs.

Within minutes the track swings right at the confluence with Black Brook. Leave the track as it fords the inflowing stream, and resume up the stream side into the trees. This is a grand corner, with tumbling stream, rocks, birch trees and bracken. **Within a couple of minutes a brace of forlorn stone shooting cabins are reached. Here double back up to the right on a well constructed path climbing to the upper limit of the trees.** At the top a grand view is revealed over the adjacent moor and clough, and north to the slopes of Black Hill.

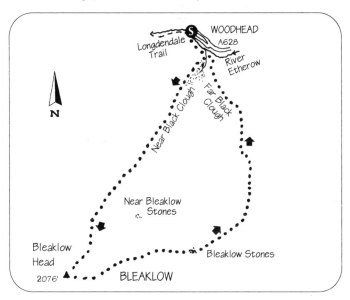

The path then turns left up the moor edge, directly above the tree line. So begins a long and splendid march onto the Bleaklow plateau. This same line carries our route for the next two miles. In the early stages it runs the full length of the wood top, affording excellent views over the wonderful environs of the Black Cloughs. **Beyond the trees the path settles down to tracing the edge of deeply cut Near Black Clough, ever gradually gaining height.** A nice little waterfall tinkling over gritstone slabs below is in marked contrast to a large windfarm back over the summit of the Woodhead road. **The brook eventually swings right and the path stays true, offering a choice of upper and lower routes for a time.**

Towards the headwaters there is an easy option to Bleaklow Stones, omitting Bleaklow Head. To take this leave the path at the point where we are nearest to the Near Bleaklow Stones, the only rocks visible, just up to the left on the skyline only a few hundred yards distant. Cross the tiny brook and strike directly up the moorland to quickly gain the outcrops. Now continue south-east for the waiting Bleaklow Stones.

The main route remains with Near Black Clough until nearing the watershed. At a bend in the now sluggish brook, a prominent cairn sits just along to the right. Here the direct path heads off at 245 degrees across a very easy, grassy way between peat tors. This continues to another cairn at the end, signalling a thinner trod rising left between enclosing peat groughs. Swinging right again over grassier terrain once more, the great pile of stones marking Bleaklow Head is gained with surprising ease.

The cairn sits on a peaty knoll, though behind it is a large, bare stony patch. To visit the Wain Stones, cross this patch to a prominent cairn, with the stones just 50 yards beyond (illustrated on page 34). **The route leaves the 'summit' cairn however by heading east along the broad watershed. A thousand footsteps might be found in the peat, but in this terrain it can mean little in navigation terms. Intermittent stakes (insufficient to be of value in poor visibility) sit on peaty knolls along the top, and certainly the highest ground, such as it is, provides the easier going: at regular intervals there is respite from the wallowing peat in the form of further sandy, firmer patches.**

An easy mistake is to err to the right and start to lose height above Alport Head: when this happens, the hassle of crossing intervening groughs at regular intervals should soon send you back on top. **Ahead, the Bleaklow Stones form an arresting skyline, and gradually then suddenly we find ourselves rising past a few boulders to gain the top.**

This proves a very pleasant oasis, the grassy plateau providing a suitable site for the weirdly sculpted rocks. Most photographed is the Anvil, a very individual rock that has featured in our sights for some considerable time: the Trident is also easily identified. This fascinating top is certainly worth a little exploration. As a viewpoint it also surpasses Bleaklow Head, with the finest features being southwards to Kinder Scout and the hills east of it, and across to the Derwent edges. Much nearer, the craggy outcrops of the Grinah Stones form a well defined nab just to the east along the ridge.

Leave by resuming east, initially with a choice of ways on a well defined drop. The main paths merge and run south of the watershed, quickly confirming their intention of gaining the Grinah Stones (see WALK 20). This is a perfectly acceptable start, even to the point of visiting them yourself. However, a study of the topography shows our aim is to turn north well before then, holding to the Derwent watershed. As such one can stick to the highest ground from leaving Bleaklow Stones, stakes being much scarcer now. If using the Grinah Stones path, break off at its low point, heading north a minute or so to regain the skyline. Continue east on the fainter watershed path.

At a stake the path makes a marked swing to the north, confirmed by a small but significant cairn: the way from here passes through a well defined, deep peat channel with a firm sandy base. Emerging at a vague fork, first clamber onto the knoll in front. Revealed is a fine view northwards, with the Barrow Stones visible over to the right.

Directly beneath the massif of Black Hill is a distinct nick in the edge of our moor. This is the point where Far Black Clough, down to the left, leaves for the valley. Either bear left to join the upper clough and a forming path; or right to stay on the Derwent watershed to descend onto a broadening ridge. After half a mile or so the next twist (right) of the watershed will be discerned, and here, if not before, bear left to find a good path tracing the rim of nearby Far Black Clough.

Follow the clough downstream a short way to the edge of the moor-top. The path then drops to quickly reach the head of a shooters' track, with the start point visible in the valley. All that remains is to follow this rapidly downhill. En route, there is some fine brook and crag scenery, constantly improving as the wooded environs of the Black Cloughs are neared. The track winds down to arrive at the ford at the foot of the cloughs, only five minutes from the starting point.

The Anvil,
Bleaklow Stones

27

5

BLEAKLOW EDGES

START *Torside*　　　　*Grid ref. SK 067983*

DISTANCE *8¼ miles*

ORDNANCE SURVEY MAPS
1:50,000
Landranger 110 - Sheffield & Huddersfield
1:25,000
Outdoor Leisure 1 - Peak District, Dark Peak

ACCESS *Start from the National Park visitor centre and car park on the B6105 on the south side of Torside Reservoir, Longdendale. Served by Summer Sunday/BH Monday Huddersfield-Glossop buses.*
● *ACCESS LAND - see page 8.*

Marvellous close-hand scenery and far reaching views over Longdendale. One or two 'rough and ready' moments make this little less genteel than a visit to the peaty heights above, but it is well worth the effort. Map and compass strongly recommended.

❺ Longdendale means reservoirs, and while not the perfect accompaniment to this ramble, they do add extra colour to the scene. The scheme to obliterate the river Etherow began in 1848 with the building of Woodhead dam. Torside, Rhodeswood, Valehouse and Bottoms reservoirs followed, to form what was then the largest man-made expanse of water in the world.

From the car park a broad path rises to join the Longdendale Trail. This runs for seven miles along the former railway between Woodhead and Hadfield. Opened in 1992, it forms the central section of the Trans-Pennine Trail, a national cycle route from Liverpool to Hull. The railway itself was the major route linking Manchester and Sheffield, but closed in 1981 (see WALK 6).

Go left for a long mile towards the dam of Woodhead Reservoir. En route we pass beneath the tumbling rocks that have rolled from the craggy edges we shall soon be tracing. Early views feature Crowden Great Brook striking into Black Hill, with Laddow Rocks prominent. Across the dam is the tiny St. James' church, otherwise known as Woodhead Chapel. Until 1961 a pub, the *George & Dragon Inn*, overlooked Woodhead Reservoir but was demolished in order to safeguard water quality.

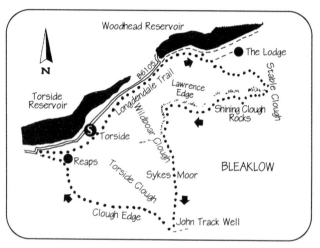

Just short of Woodhead dam, take a stile on the right to join a parallel farm road. Go left past decaying red-brick railway cottages and remain on this drive. This was the site of Crowden's tiny railway station, which closed in 1957. Over to the left waggons rumble over Woodhead Bridge, crossing a northern arm of the reservoir. **The drive runs to a cattle-grid at the approach to The Lodge Farm. Don't cross, but turn up to the right with the fence. A vague way climbs to a stile at a fence crossroads, then curve left above a pond curiously decorated by ornamental shrubbery.**

From a stile in the rising fence cross to another stile in this odd corner then turn upstream with Shining Clough and shortly cross it to a fence corner opposite. Again turn along the fence top, rough terrain leading along to intercept a shooters' track (a former quarry track) rising out of the pastures.

Turn up this for a surprisingly short climb to near the base of the first rocks. At a gate the track forks. The branch right quickly falters in the amphitheatre beneath the crags, but there are many non-scrambling routes up onto the edge. The left branch, through the gate, is a horrendously bulldozed scar on what was a delightful path in the finest upper reaches of Stable Clough. Illegally constructed in 1993 for easier access to the poor grouse, the ground is due to be re-instated. If it has by the time you pass, then it may be as nice to continue up the clough onto the moortop. At the top a stile to the right admits back onto the moor. Slant right to drop down to the edge.

Torside Clough across Torside Reservoir

However gaining the edge, pause to inspect the intimidating buttresses of Dowstone Rocks. Known to climbers as Shining Clough Rocks, these offer major challenges to those rock athletes who still appreciate crags that take a bit of effort to reach. **Leaving, head off to the west skirting some grand declivities as you go.** Throughout this section - indeed the entire walk - the slopes of Black Hill sprawl across Longdendale. **Shining Clough's deep ravine quickly interrupts progress, and the way is forced inland to negotiate it. Resuming, a generally clear path treads the mixed terrain where peat moor meets gritstone edge.**

It is fine walking all the way, passing above Deer Knowl and then rising over Lawrence Edge before reaching the particularly scattered jumble of rocks that is the Rollick Stones. An easier rise leads

above these craggy walls to approach **Wildboar Clough.** Below are wide views down over Torside Reservoir with Rhodeswood Reservoir below it. **A good path forges on up this deeper enclave, though here we have no aim to get back on the other side. Continue up the clear path as the clough abates, shadowed by a sturdy fence on the other side.**

Regular stiles tempt us to cross, but remain with the brook for some considerable time until fence and brook take a sharp turn left. Though the extended fence climbs higher up the moor, leave it here by either the preceding stile or one on the very bend, this being notable as the path also crosses here to leave fence and brook behind. The path, incidentally, is striking directly up towards the summit, intercepting the Pennine Way path en route for an easy passage to the top, should you feel so inclined.

Otherwise, leave the path and set a bearing virtually due south, entailing a half-mile crossing of the untracked Sykes Moor and aiming for the easily identified confluence at John Track Well. At this very point the Pennine Way is joined, an unmistakable path on the south side of Wildboar Grain (not to be confused with the Wildboar Clough we have just left). Here the path crosses the other sidestream and turns sharply north-west to run above the brook. The well itself is located just above the confluence. Even if not landing directly on the spot, erring a little either side will still bring you to the stream and the path on its opposite bank.

Crossing at the confluence turn right on the PW on its descent from Bleaklow. Aided initially by modern path repairs in the form of crazy paving and winding flags, these soon halt and the firm path gets on with the business of skirting the rim of the rapidly unfolding Torside Clough. This superb path now enjoys a memorable mile on Clough Edge. Ahead is Reaps Farm with Torside Reservoir in the bottom, backed by the great sprawl of Black Hill. **At the end the path descends to leave the access area, the final steep stage sees a pitched stone path winding down to a stile. The path then goes left to approach Reaps Farm, slanting down above it to follow its drive out towards the B6105 at a former level crossing.**

Just short of the road a PW link path turns down to join the Longdendale Trail by the roadside. Simply turn right for ten minutes to return to the start point above the car park.

6

THE WAIN STONES

START *Old Glossop*   *Grid ref. SK 042947*

DISTANCE *9 miles*

ORDNANCE SURVEY MAPS
1:50,000
Landranger 110 - Sheffield & Huddersfield
1:25,000
Outdoor Leisure 1 - Peak District, Dark Peak

ACCESS *Start from the 'village' of Old Glossop, half a mile east of Glossop town centre. Parking near the foot of Shepley Street, before the large factory (Glossop Super Alloys). Served by bus from Glossop. Glossop is served by train from Manchester and bus from almost anywhere. • ACCESS AREA - see page 8.*

A splendid approach to Bleaklow's broad tops, matched by a leisurely return through Shelf Brook. Map and compass strongly recommended.

S   Old Glossop is a charming, independent little village, comprising numerous attractive old houses with mullioned windows, and cottages grouped around the dominant church with its spire. It also has a Post office, village cross and a pub, the *Queens Arms*.

Walk past the factory and the bus turning circle and along the rough lane. To the right the part-wooded knoll of Shire Hill is prominent. **As the lane emerges into a field, take a stile on the left to climb the field-side path to Open Country, which is gained immediately from the stile at the top.** Looking back, Glossop leads the eye to further urban sprawl; better to focus on the mixed country nearer to hand, and the sweeping moorland over the Snake Road.

A clear path heads straight up the grassy ridge-end of Lightside, through a couple of collapsed walls. A fence with the second wall is the point where the direct climbing path (now through heather) can be varied by going a few yards right to trace the rim of a well-defined edge with a number of fair individual outcrops.

Ahead now our mountain asserts its stature, and well ahead beyond the head of the clough, the three Wain Stones pierce the skyline - a useful guide as they are virtually on the summit. **In time the path joins in on the edge. With intimidating peat groughs on the left, remain on the 'edge' as the path fades, working round to find a forlorn fence above Yellowslacks Brook. Now the Yellowslacks edge takes shape, its cliffs lining the head of Dowstone Clough.**

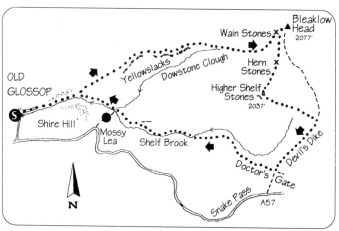

Simply contour round to the head of the ravine, and continue on a path shadowing the moorland brook. In parts the bed (if dry enough) can be traced, its slabby floor affording sound progress. Be in no hurry to vacate this easy passage, for all round is much rougher stuff! At a confluence of like sikes the inevitable can be put off no longer, so climb left up to the prow of a suitable peat grough to locate the Wain Stones over to the left, and make the best of this final section.

Though of modest scale and few in number, the Wain Stones are a famous Bleaklow landmark, the celebrated pairing known as *The Kiss* being aptly named. Up here however, the shelter they offer may be

33

more valued than the romance! **Beyond the stones a prominent cairn points the way on to join the Pennine Way for the final yards to the summit.** The highest ground is a surprisingly pleasant spot, a sprawling cairn being perched on peat across a dry, stony, plateau. If higher ground seems to rise further east ignore it - it's an illusion - isn't it? The view, inevitably for such a vast plateau, is unexceptional, being limited to distant prospects only, including the Holme Moss mast on Black Hill to the north.

The Wain Stones: a snatched Kiss at dusk

Leave by re-crossing the dry plateau, seeking out the route marked by yellow blobs and PW markers. The yellow refers to the classic Marsden-Edale Walk, which in any case coincides with the PW hereabouts. **This turns south before reaching the Wain Stones: note that the PW has been re-routed here, now charting a well defined course initially through deep peat channels. It is regularly waymarked, thus by-passing the old line (south to the prominent Hern Stones). Certainly the PW offers the easiest route off the Bleaklow plateau, but if conditions are suitable a finer alternative exists via the Hern Stones to Higher Shelf Stones, the distinct rise to the south-west.**

On gaining the Hern Stones, strike out for the prominent, more inviting rise of Higher Shelf Stones. The peat groughs gradually diminish, to rise to the top. If trending to the left (east) side of the top you are likely to encounter extensive aircraft wreckage. A plaque erected in 1988 commemorates the 40th anniversary of a disastrous crash in which all 13 crew members of a US Air Force reconnaissance plane were killed.

The summit is found 200 yards to the west, at 2037ft/621m. Here a white-painted Ordnance column (S2627) sits on a solid gritstone plinth, above a crowd of shapely outcrops, the stones themselves. This more attractive setting brings a far superior view to Bleaklow's main top, including the inviting Doctor's Gate path down Shelf Brook, the Snake Pass road and the head of the Woodlands Valley. Lower Shelf Stones are just around the rim, while the long northern edges of Kinder Scout stand out southwards.

While the Doctor's Gate path far below is our objective, the more rewarding route is more circuitous: from here a very prominent dike can be seen pointing south-east beyond intervening Crooked Clough. Aiming for it, a sketchy trod materialises to lead to the clough, followed by similarly easy going on a path with the dike to rejoin the PW at Devil's Dike under Alport Low.

Turn right along the deep incision of the dike - its bed now transformed into a more durable route by PW work. Later a short flagged section is followed by a firm surface leading out to the road: as it seems we are about to meet the road, the conspicuous line of Doctor's Gate is met, a crossroads with a more traditional green path. This is a former packhorse route created in the mid-16th century by one Dr. Talbot, vicar of Glossop. It provided a sound route for the trading link between the Woodlands Valley and Glossop, and its importance is identified by the stone surface on the opening section. **Here escape the PW by turning right along the more inviting part-sunken paved section.**

Within a couple of minutes a short, steep zigzag descent is made to cheery Urchin Clough, followed by a graceful sweep down to the floor of Shelf Brook. Since leaving Higher Shelf Stones its outline has constantly improved, becoming especially aggressive (along with Lower Shelf Stones) as height is lost.

In the folds of the hills a memorial footbridge crosses the brook, which is shadowed for a while before pulling round to meet a track in front of a barn. This drops down towards Mossy Lea Farm. At the track junction before it take the right-hand bridge over Yellowslacks Brook. To the right is a brief glimpse up into Dowstone Clough. **This same track runs on through the fields to soon regain the outer route for the final minutes.**

7

COOMBES EDGE

START *Rowarth*   *Grid ref. SK 011892*

DISTANCE *5¾ miles*

ORDNANCE SURVEY MAPS
1:50,000
Landranger 110 - Sheffield & Huddersfield
1:25,000
Outdoor Leisure 1 - Peak District, Dark Peak

ACCESS *Start from the village centre. There is a car park at the entrance. Alternative, more accessible starts are found at the junction by Plumstead Farm, on the Monk's Road off the A624 (this also puts the pub halfway round). There are bus services within a mile of the route at Charlesworth and Little Hayfield.*

Easy walking on old green ways and fieldpaths, with the focal point being a superb skyline walk. There are fine views towards Kinder Scout and the high moors.

S Rowarth is a very attractive little village well off the beaten track. Its finest feature is the pub, sat beneath the village and ideally placed at the end of the walk.

From the car park head into the village. At the main corner is an L-shaped arrangement of houses; on the left is Drinkwater's Buildings of 1812, while a 1797 datestone adorns a house on the right. **At this corner go straight ahead a few yards along the broad track. Almost at once a path rises left between gardens, thereafter climbing pleasantly on a part sunken old way up the field-side.** At once there are grand views back south and east to Chinley Churn, Lantern Pike and the western edges of Kinder.

At the top a stile admits onto a junction of ways. Go left through the gateway but then leave the green wall-side track by tracing the one slanting up the field. This rises delightfully up the centre of this rough grazing, passing some patches of gorse as its course becomes thinner. Higher up it re-asserts itself to rise to a stile at the top. The way continues up the wall-side. To the left now are far-reaching views over the vast metropolis of greater Manchester.

As the wall drops away a fence takes over. The old trackway goes beyond the fence-stile, slanting down to the house at Near Slack. An alternative simply stays with the fence. Level with the house, the lower path sends a branch back up to a stile in the fence. However reached, from this stile bear up the pasture on the well defined green way, rising to a stile and gate in the next wall. The way resumes through a further pasture, just past which it crosses rough moorland to a crossroads with a broad bridleway on its summit.

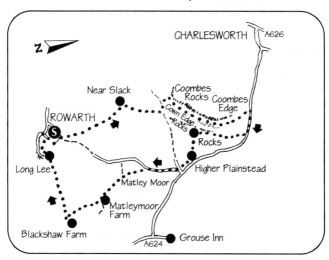

Go left to the next corner and leave the track by a stile on the right. Officially the path descends to the bottom corner to gain the foot of Coombes Rocks, though a thoughtfully provided courtesy stile in the fence across the top gives direct access to the footpath on the edge, avoiding folk wandering all over the field. This is a stupendous moment as the true edge of Coombes Rocks is gained. Beneath is a great bowl of colourful country, with a tumble of boulders frowning down. **Our way simply turns right along the crest, soon encountering sizeable crags. At the point where a strip plantation is reached on the right, a sturdy pinnacle can be seen rising from the rocks below. The path forges on, sheer delight as Coombes Edge is traversed.**

Beyond the trees a track comes in from the right, accessed by the first of two stiles. At the second, a sunken green lane doubles back right to effect a short-cut to Cown Edge Rocks. **The main route moves on to the parallel track, which moves slightly away from the abating edge between crumbling wall and fence. This soon swings right to cross to the Monk's Road.** This offers a stunning bird's-eye view over the Glossop environs and across to Black Hill and Bleaklow.

Turn right along the road for a couple of minutes then take a narrow fenced path climbing back onto the moor. Levelling out it runs on the very crest of the moorland ridge. At more than 1345ft/410m this is the highest point of Cown Edge. **Passing a quarry the path runs on to meet a green track through a stile.** This is the short-cut path mentioned. **Advance along this past further smaller quarrying sites and through increasingly rocky surrounds of the edge. At a fork slant left down to Rocks Farm. A stile gives access to a short green way, going round the house and out along the drive. This runs through Higher Plainstead Farm and out onto the Monk's Road again.**

Without setting foot on the road, take a stile on the right and descend the field to a stile in the bottom right corner. At the junction here take the road straight ahead, rising steadily to a corner. Take the stile ahead onto Matley Moor, and enjoy a grand stride over this lovely heather-clad pocket moor. Fine views ahead lead down the valley past Rowarth, and to Lantern Pike with Chinley Churn behind. **The green path slants down to the left to a corner stile onto a rough lane. Go left, staying on the track which opens out then becomes enclosed again to reach Matleymoor Farm. Keep straight on the broader track, passing another farm drive before a sharp bend with Blackshaw Farm just down to the left. Here go straight ahead onto a corner of rough pasture, with Lantern Pike (see WALK 9) just ahead.**

At the multiple guidepost step over the fence on the right by the post, and head across the field. Join a wall on the right and go on to the crumbling corner. A faint path continues, angling away from the stream down to the right and on into the next field beyond a wall

corner. Forge on to the narrowing far end, and from the gate head down the field-sides on a rough track towards Long Lee Farm. Note the path is on this side of the wall, not the other as per map.

Long Lee,
Rowarth

At a 1926 guidepost don't go down the last field-side to the farm, but turn right along the wall-side (path diverted). At the first chance go left and down the wall-side outside the farm's environs. Long Lee is a superb farmstead with a 1663 datestone and featuring mullioned windows and an austere, part forlorn look. **Past the farmhouse wall corner continue down the field to a ladder-stile, then go right down the field-side again. Veer left towards the end to find a tiny foot-bridge on the stream (beneath a little milldam), just across which is a rough lane. By turning right this leads back up to the village, but by turning left you will be faced by the *Little Mill Inn*.**

This fascinating watering hole dates from 1781. It is a hugely welcoming spot with splendid ale and a good kids' playground, but beyond these fine features are two rather special ones. To one side of the building is a restored 'Derbyshire Bell' Pullman railway carriage, and at the other a fully working, very large waterwheel. You can't forego all this! **Turn back up the lane to finish, either by road or bridleway.**

8

CRACKEN EDGE

START Hayfield   Grid ref. SK 035869

DISTANCE 7 miles

ORDNANCE SURVEY MAPS
1:50,000
Landranger 110 - Sheffield & Huddersfield
1:25,000
Outdoor Leisure 1 - Peak District, Dark Peak

ACCESS Start from the village centre. There is a large car park at the start of the Sett Valley Trail. Served by bus from Glossop and Stockport, and more distantly on Summer Sundays/BH Mondays.

A rich variety of interest on the western limits of the Dark Peak. Good moorland surrounds and excellent distant views, with Kinder Scout particularly well seen.

S Built around the mountain stream of the river Sett, Hayfield has a charming village centre with old inns and cottages providing some attractive corners. St. Matthew's church is centrally placed, having been rebuilt in 1818 after being destroyed by floods. The village street was by-passed in modern times by the Glossop-Chapel road. The former railway from New Mills has been converted into a three-mile trail for walkers and cyclists: ironic that a line that brought folk in their thousands from the big city to the country, now entices them to stroll back the other way! There is little sign of Hayfield's industrious past, today's visitor will encounter more coffee shops than cotton mills.

There is an information booth at the old station car park, open weekends. A plaque placed on the wall in 1994 commemorates the centenary of the Peak & Northern Footpaths Society and the establishment of the historic Hayfield-Snake path. Formerly the long-winded Peak District & Northern Counties Footpaths Preservation Society, their footpath signs are to be found all around the district, but are particularly profuse in the High Peak. Many are of great historic interest, augmented by some attractive modern additions.

From the car park return up Station Road, cross straight over past St. John's Methodist Church and up Chapel Street (becoming Meadows Road). At the top a rougher drive continues up beyond the houses. This is Ridge Top Lane, which climbs to a bend into a small patch of open country. Here continue up a few yards to a stile on the left, from where a footpath contours off through the fields. This delightful path affords superb views over Hayfield to Lantern Pike and beyond, and more interestingly east to Kinder Scout. **At the end it enters trees to approach Phoside Farm.**

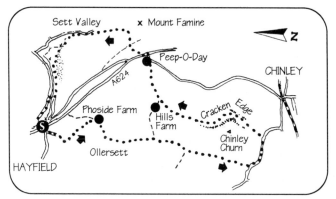

Pass along the front of the house to a bridle-gate above a barn, then take the path climbing Foxholes Clough. This attractive wooded dell has an old mill ruin down to the left, with its millpond just above. **The path climbs pleasantly out of the trees. Ignore a fork left over the brook, and continue up to the top of the wall. As it bends away another fork is reached, this time take that doubling back left up onto the open moor. Towards the top it runs faintly on to a crossroads with a broader track on the moorland of Ollersett.**

Turn left on this track above the beginnings of the brook, running to and then with an old wall. This soon reaches a junction of tracks and old walls: take the enclosed green way straight ahead. This runs on

41

with increasingly extensive views to the right over New Mills and Whaley Bridge and back across to greater Manchester. **Emerging the track continues with an old wall, a splendid stride before becoming enclosed again. This broad green way slants gradually down to eventually absorb vehicle tracks to debouch onto a road.**

Cracken Edge, looking to Kinder Scout

Go left on this quiet country lane, still savouring those views as it turns to descend towards Chinley. Part way down take a stile on the left to enter a colourful gorse pasture. An old hollowed pathway heads away, rising ever gradually beneath the first signs of Cracken Edge Quarries. Beyond a stile the way continues unfailingly, a delight to follow as it runs beneath more extensive quarried cliffs.

Remain on this main path, still hollowed as it rises to a stile. Beyond here it runs a level course past extensive spoil heaps and ruins under the edge. When a higher level path drops down, look over to the left to see a small cave in a corner hollow, and look over the drop to the right to see abandoned winding gear. **This outstanding green path runs on yet again, contouring beneath further quarrying to eventually leave the site behind. It then winds down above the solitary house of Whiterakes and down to meet the Hills Farm road. Turn right on this, down to join a back lane at Peep-O-Day. Advance to the main road at its summit, cross and go left on the verge.**

At the first chance turn right up a rough lane alongside a house. This rises past a heather tract to a guidepost at a junction. Almost opposite, a bridle-gate sends a field-side path heading away, continuing on to a gate above the upper Sett Valley. This reveals a classic prospect of Kinder, along its western flanks with Kinderlow End prominent opposite, and farms and fields beneath the brown edge. The path winds down to the left, becoming firmer as it runs on to meet a farm road.

South Head and Mount Famine from the upper Sett Valley

Go left a few steps only on the farm road then take a bridleway across to a bridle-gate beneath a wood. This track runs on to Stones House Farm, dropping down to its left and resuming along the bottom of the wood. At the end it meets the river Sett and then the end of a drive. Just after a merging of such ways, double back down to a footbridge in front of a cottage, then downstream a short way before the snicket climbs onto the Kinder Road. Go left along here to quickly return to the centre of Hayfield. A subway near the church will return you to the car park without having to cross the busy by-pass road.

LANTERN PIKE

START *Hayfield*   *Grid ref. SK 035869*

DISTANCE *6 miles*

ORDNANCE SURVEY MAPS
1:50,000
Landranger 110 - Sheffield & Huddersfield
1:25,000
Outdoor Leisure 1 - Peak District, Dark Peak

ACCESS *Start from the village centre. There is a large car park at the start of the Sett Valley Trail. Served by bus from Glossop and Stockport, and more distantly on Summer Sundays/BH Mondays.*

An easy walk to a local viewpoint, returning by a colourful corner of Kinder moorland. For a note on Hayfield see WALK 8.

⑤   **Leave the car park by the far end, where the Sett Valley Trail sets off along the old railway line.** Earlier maps depict it as a permissive footpath but it is now a public bridleway. The cul-de-sac railway from New Mills closed in 1970 only two years after reaching its centenary. Imaginatively saved from obscurity and converted into a three-mile trail for walkers and cyclists, it is ironic that the line that brought folk in their thousands from the big city to the country now entices them to stroll back the other way! Though not a classic railway walk it is nevertheless ideal for our purposes.

Follow this for rather less than a mile, and at the far end of Birch Vale Reservoir turn down to the right at a crossroads with a footpath immediately before a plastics factory. The path runs across the dam to a footbridge over the river Sett. From the bridge a thin path surmounts the brow and rises to the top right corner of the field. Here a field-side path climbs to join a drive. Turn up to the left and

follow this drive as it zigzags up onto a road. During the climb there are fine views eastwards to the western edges of Kinder Scout, also Chinley Churn over the reservoir below.

At the road cross to a surfaced drive up the side of the little terrace of Windy Knowl, and follow it steeply to its terminus at a house. A broad track takes over, rising more gently to encounter heather moorland. At the following gate we enter the open country of Lantern Pike. This small patch of moorland is one of the National Trust's lesser known properties, a valued oasis among the fields.

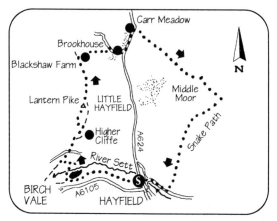

The bridleway runs along the base of the moor, but the finest route takes the wall-side path back up to the left. On the brow it swings right to enjoy a grand saunter along the heathery edge to the highest point at 1224ft/373m. By this stage the modest outcrops have abated, but the top is marked by a topograph describing the full panorama. It was erected in 1950 in memory of Edwin Royce, a stalwart access campaigner. Cown Edge appears to the north, with Little Hayfield down below on the main road.

The path continues by gently declining back to the far corner of the moor. Here the bridleway drops down between walls to enter a large tract of rough pasture. The path swings around to the left to drop to a multiple guidepost on the edge of a rough lane on a bend. Turn right here to Blackshaw Farm, remaining on the track round the left of the buildings to meet the drive. This leads down the fields (parallel

path) to merge into a lane. Turn right through Brookhouse and up onto the main road. Brookhouse is a select little hamlet featuring a splendid large house with mullioned windows and another in an old mill.

Turn left along the A624 for a few nervous minutes, and escape with relief at a gate (and 1905 guidepost) into Open Country on the right opposite Carr Meadow Farm. Instantly we are upon colourful country on the very western flanks of Kinder. A broad track heads away, but leave within yards by dropping to a footbridge on Hollingworth Clough. An idyllic spot, the grassy bank of the tinkling brook would be a paddling and picnic honeypot were there car parking available on the nearby road!

The broad path rises up the slope behind, with a wall soon coming to join us. This easy rise is soon concluded on the brow, and as the wall parts company the path bears off left across Middle Moor. Ahead are Kinder Low and the twin peaks of South Head and Mount Famine. **On crossing another clough a re-seeded section leads on to a curiously sited but much appreciated bridge over a severely reedy section.** If you were wondering about the notice back at the gate off the road, now you know why!

Over to the left is a white shooting cabin. With its adjacent hut it is a prominent sight from many local viewpoints. **Just past the bridge is a crossroads of ways and an old guidepost.** This even advises our altitude, a modest 1090ft. Just ahead, Kinder's western slopes are well seen now, and one could advance a little further along the path for a better view. **Turn right at the junction on an equally broad path running across to a wall corner.** This is the true Snake Path, an historic route bound from Hayfield for the Woodlands Valley by way of William and Ashop Cloughs: it was opened in 1897. **Just along the wall-side it leaves the moor (and Open Country) at a kissing-gate.**

The track swings left around a rougher pasture and from the far corner it works down through the fields, largely with iron kissing-gates confirming the way alongside other gates. Hayfield soon appears below and the way leads unerringly down, sometimes with evidence of its earlier sunken course. At the bottom it becomes enclosed and drops to emerge between houses onto Kinder Road on the edge of Hayfield. Turn right to finish. A white house on the left was Hayfield Grammar School, built in 1719 (founded in 1604).

10

KINDER DOWNFALL

START *Hayfield*   *Grid ref. SK 048869*

DISTANCE *11 miles*

ORDNANCE SURVEY MAPS
1:50,000
Landranger 110 - Sheffield & Huddersfield
1:25,000
Outdoor Leisure 1 - Peak District, Dark Peak

ACCESS *Start from the Bowden Bridge car park, a mile along Bank Street/Kinder Road from the village centre. As this rapidly fills on any decent day, you may have to work back towards or into Hayfield to park (large car park at start of Sett Valley Trail). Hayfield is served by bus from Glossop and Stockport, and more distantly on Summer Sundays/BH Mondays. • ACCESS LAND - see page 8.*

A lengthy stride around the western extremities of Kinder Scout's upper reaches. There is much of interest all around, although Kinder Downfall will always be the great draw. Map and compass strongly recommended. For a note on Hayfield please refer to WALK 8.

S Bowden Bridge is steeped in the history of the outdoors movement, for from this spot the main body of heroes set forth to begin the celebrated 'Mass Trespass' of 1932, culminating in five of its number serving prison sentences. A plaque on the quarry wall was unveiled in 1982 on the anniversary of this memorable gesture (see page 3). All who walk upon Kinder's hallowed ground should seek out the story behind the trespass (try reading *Freedom to Roam* by Howard Hill) to be aware of both the need for it, and ultimately its success in helping win the freedom (by and large) of Kinder today. The campsite shop sells maps and refreshments: there is a ranger base attached. The *Sportsman* pub stands just back along the road towards Hayfield.

From the car park cross the road and the bridge and go left up the parallel road. Swinging right, keep right as a farm road branches left. Slanting gently right to another fork, don't cross the cattle-grid but take the lesser branch right at the National Trust sign. A slender farm road rises away. South Head and Mount Famine increase in grandeur ahead (see illustration on page 43), seemingly exciting peaks! **On a brow leave the road as it turns downhill, and bear right along a firm, level track. This soon rises up the hillside bound for those shapely peaks, becoming greener as it curves up to a gate in the ridge wall.**

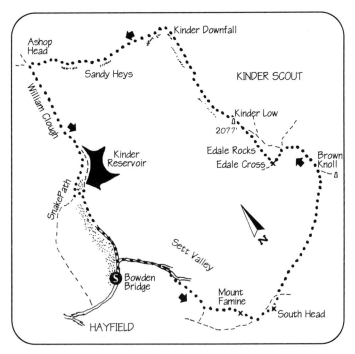

Without passing through, a ladder-stile in the corner to the left gives direct access to Mount Famine: though regularly used to gain the access area, it is not a public footpath. A couple of pastures with crumbling walls lead onto steeper slopes, where a path winds up to easier ground. Briefly forking, the left branch traces the rim, merging at the top where a narrow way runs on to the highest point

above small outcrops. This is a stunning viewpoint with the upper Sett Valley deep beneath our planned skyline walk. **South Head also waits, so keep straight on the edge path, dropping to the saddle where a broad track (an old road) passes through. A slim green path breaks off to scale the easy slope of South Head, crowned by a cairn.**

Drop back down the other side of South Head to rejoin the main track where it swings off to the right. At this important junction a signposted path goes off left to descend to the upper Sett, but our way is the broader path between the two, heading along the wide ridge towards Brown Knoll. Ahead, Kinder's features include Swine's Back, with Pym Chair and the Pagoda discerned behind. **The path remains clear, following a wall along the occasionally marshy top.**

In time the path rises as a firm grassy way amongst increasingly peaty surrounds. Fence replaces wall and peatier terrain is encountered on the brow. A branch path right to the Ordnance Survey column on Brown Knoll is unworthy of a detour, so swing left on the main path as it cuts a corner of fence and old wall. Part-way along it becomes flagged, leading comfortably on in this fashion to a crossroads with the Hayfield-Edale track under Swine's Back.

Through the gate a firm path climbs beneath Swine's Back, while the track right quickly arrives at Jacob's Ladder for a descent into the Vale of Edale. **For added interest go left along the track for two minutes to Edale Cross.** On the summit of the historic Hayfield-Edale path, this medieval waymarker (see page 1) stands preserved in a wall shelter, useful on a rough day before gaining the plateau. The date 1810 refers to a restoration: it stands where three wards of the former Royal Forest of the Peak met. **Alongside it, a stile sends a wall-side path climbing past outcrops up to the right, then leaves the wall as it rises past the rocks. Suddenly a flagged surface takes over to lead up the moor.**

A junction is reached with a path going out to the cairn on Kinderlow End. On our path are scant remains of a shooting cabin. Just to the right Edale Rocks tempt a detour: if taken, the Pennine Way then leads up to rejoin us on Kinder Low. **Otherwise continue up the path to its demise on the top, where a couple of sprawling cairns encourage us on: just beyond is Kinder Low.** Several shapely, wind-eroded rocks occupy a dry sandy floor, one supporting an Ordnance Survey column (S4113). At 2077ft/633m it is the summit of this walk, and only 10ft lower than the highest point of Kinder Scout. **From here either go left to the edge or follow a sandy path running north to gain the edge.**

Now simply go north along the western rim with a firm, undulating path underfoot and much of interest all around. From the outset Kinder Reservoir and environs appear, and remain so throughout. Almost at once keen eyes will see the two tiny remains of an aircraft wreck just off the path. **On we go, absorbing a path coming up to join us at the distinct crossing of Red Brook.** This is a good vantage point for Mermaid's Pool on the slopes below. **Before long this grand walk arrives at the highlight, Kinder Downfall.** Not that the Downfall itself is fully evident without clambering cautiously about to get a view.

Kinder Downfall

This is a classic moment as a mild moorland stream - the Kinder river - reaches a dramatic conclusion on the very edge of the plateau. Rimmed by boulders and crags, this wild place is known throughout

Peakland, indeed walking circles throughout the land. If the day be windy, then the first sighting is of the 'upfall', as the waters are blown back over the edge. Reposing walkers on grassy surrounds, fending off hungry sheep, emphasise the status of this locale.

Cross the stony bed of the stream safely above the Downfall, and resume the edge walk. The mighty rocks above Kinder Buttress offer sites for a good sojourn and better prospect of the Downfall environs. **The path forges on, passing along Sandy Heys and through boulders above Upper Western Buttress. Suddenly the end is reached at a profound drop above Ashop Head, marked by a sprawling cairn.** Just beneath us to the left is Mill Hill Rocks buttress, of which we remain unaware, while ahead is a brief sighting of Black Hill and Bleaklow.

A stone pitched path winds down the steep end and on to a cross-roads with the Snake Path at Ashop Head, and an attractive modern marker post. Go left, the Snake Path running gently on before sudden arrival at the top of an eroded section: descend with caution. Tracing the Snake Path down William Clough we follow in the footsteps of the Mass Trespassers of 1932. This book's publication marks the centenary of the opening of the Snake Path, an event that would be perfectly celebrated by seeing it suitably restored. **This shaley section is soon over and a contrastingly narrow path settles down to an absorbing journey through William Clough, crossing and re-crossing the stream.** The way is sheer delight, though be aware of potential for landslips. **Eventually, at the last re-crossing, path and stream emerge into more open surrounds.**

With Kinder Reservoir just ahead now, the path immediately forks. The easiest way goes left with the stream, soon entering a permissive path along the reservoir wall. **More interestingly take the contouring right branch, which makes a brief climb before resuming a level march along White Brow.** It enjoys fine views over the reservoir to the our edges walk and across to South Head and Mount Famine. **Running above a scattered wood the way reaches a broader track coming down from the right.** If starting from the village, it is easier to go along this, the true Snake Path, to finish (see the conclusion of WALK 9).

Turn down the track through a gateway to descend to the reservoir wall and lower path. Go right, down to the reservoir access road. This leads back to the car park, though better to immediately take the Kinder river footbridge on the left and follow a broad woodland path downstream, merging into a drive to run back out onto the road.

11

CROWDEN CLOUGH

START *Edale* *Grid ref. SK 108847*

DISTANCE *6 miles*

ORDNANCE SURVEY MAPS
1:50,000
Landranger 110 - Sheffield & Huddersfield
1:25,000
Outdoor Leisure 1 - Peak District, Dark Peak

ACCESS Start from Barber Booth, a mile west of Edale village. There is a National Park car park just along the 'no through road' towards Upper Booth. Edale is served by Manchester-Sheffield trains and Summer Sunday/BH Monday buses from Hayfield, Chesterfield and Castleton. • ACCESS AREA - see page 8.

A fine, contrasting walk. Crowden Clough stylishly penetrates the flanks of Kinder Scout, while the middle section of the walk negotiates the peat groughs that defend the summit of the National Park. If conditions deteriorate, this upper section of the ramble can easily be omitted. Map and compass strongly recommended.

S Barber Booth car park sits beneath colourful, recolonised spoil heaps that are a result of the building of the Cowburn Tunnel. Completed in 1893, it burrows deep under the moor to re-emerge a good couple of miles distant. **From the car park head back along the road for two minutes towards the 4-arched railway bridge, then turn left over an arched wooden bridge on the river Noe. A path rises to join a farm track, going left until expiring after a couple of fields.**

A thin path takes over, crossing via successive stiles to the far corner. Above us are the flanks of Grindslow Knoll, with the Crowden Tower heights ahead, while Edale Rocks are on the skyline directly ahead.

On along a field side the path aims directly for Upper Booth, just ahead. Several fields are crossed to arrive at the hamlet. Take the gate behind the first house, then left down through the farmyard and out onto the road. This attractive hamlet features a postbox within the farmyard, and one of the many camping barns now available as inexpensive accommodation in the Peak.

Go right to the bridge on Crowden Brook then take a stile upstream. A good path heads up and then outside the clough, enjoying lovely scenery as a preamble to gaining the open hill. When the path drops to cross a tiny footbridge on the beck, one last pasture remains before a stile into Open Country. This is a splendid moment with the clough leading the eye up to the craggy Crowden Tower, making a well-timed appearance on the skyline at its head.

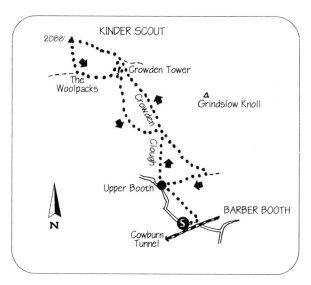

The path presents easy walking as it heads away up the stream side. Very early on a path merges in from the right - we shall use this towards the end of the walk. **In time the going becomes a little rougher and the path makes several crossings of the stream.** During this spell there are some lovely little waterfalls and deep pools: indeed a hot summer's day in the heat of the clough could see one's progress irrevocably falter at these temptations! Another surprise is a large holly, far and away the highest tree up the clough. **As the gradient increases and the boulder-choked stream takes on a ravine-like character, a path escapes left for a direct climb to Crowden Tower. Far better, however, to remain on the thinner clough path up the left side - other perhaps than in times of spate.**

Crowden Clough,
looking to
Crowden Tower

Forge on up, in dry spells easier progress being to take to the gritstone steps of the stream bed. In the upper reaches this becomes the obvious way, and a fine little scramble can be enjoyed negotiating a series of rock steps to meet the contouring edge path. This climbs left to the top of the Tower, the way to go if Kinder's summit holds no appeal.

For the full itinerary continue straight up the left arm of the clough, which initially retains its character in the form of a chaotic pile of great boulders ahead. A path skirts round to the right, but inside, scramblers will find a way up a chimney to the right. Beyond here the way settles down until the rocks fade away and the path runs on, still rising clearly. Crowden Tower's summit rocks are back to the left and the Woolpacks' Pagoda and Pym Chair prominent just further along.

At a fork keep left on a gentler rise away from the edge rocks. Quite quickly you should arrive at a sturdy cairn on a solid patch of ground due north of Pym Chair and the Woolpacks. The summit cairn sits about 230 yards to the west, enclosing a stake and clearly visible across a sea of peat. At 2088ft/636m this is not only the crown of the National Park, but the highest independent summit entirely in England south of Fountains Fell in the Yorkshire Dales (though there is higher ground in the Black Mountains on the Welsh Border).

Surprisingly, given the nature of Kinder's plateau, there is a view to be had. The only worthwhile picture is southwards, where the ground falls most markedly to the edge, revealing many features of the heart of Peakland. Otherwise only distant landmarks feature, such as cooling towers to the north-west and the Holme Moss mast to the north. **It is the more appealing southerly direction we take to return to sanity. Pym Chair and the Woolpacks make an obvious target, but anything remotely south is going to deposit you safely on the broad edge path. Very quickly the peaty ground relents and easier going leads gently down to the edge.**

Go left to gain the rocks overlooking the Woolpacks, and prepare to spend time exploring. The most substantial group of rocks feature the Pagoda (which can be scaled with ease), overlooking the valley. Here we are looking down on Edale Head, Jacob's Ladder and Youngate Bridge at its foot. At the 'moor' side of our immediate rocks, the shapely stones of Pym Chair (illustrated on page 65) are prominent.

The main path (there are several variants) continues east across the moor, into the heart of the Woolpacks. Any number of formations can be located and named in this absorbing wonderland also known as Whipsnade. **Beyond them the path resumes for a couple of minutes to the rocky crest of Crowden Tower. After admiring the view into Crowden Clough, go left on the path down to the head of the clough, where we emerged. This time however, turn sharp right without crossing the stream, on a splendid trod contouring beneath the Tower and out onto the edge of the broad southern ridge.**

A broader path runs along this edge above a few outcrops. When it swings right at the end, drop left to a crumbling wall below, and go right with it, down the slope. This leads quickly over pleasant terrain down into the clough, remaining with the descending wall at a junction of such walls. Cross the stream to regain the outward path.

Turning downstream one could retrace those early steps to finish. **For variety and interest the following option is recommended. At the path fork just ahead, bear left on that rising to meet the wall and onto the brow. It continues on above a small wood then contours around the base of the moor.** This spell affords super views across the green pastures of the upper Vale of Edale to the Mam Tor ridge. **At an Open Country notice at Broadlee-bank, drop right to a stile onto the Pennine Way. Double back down this through the fields to return to Upper Booth, now retracing the opening steps or simply following the quiet road back.**

The Pagoda, Kinder Scout

12

RUSHUP EDGE & MAM TOR

START *Edale* *Grid ref. SK 123852*

DISTANCE *7½ miles*

ORDNANCE SURVEY MAPS
1:50,000
Landranger 110 - Sheffield & Huddersfield
1:25,000
Outdoor Leisure 1 - Peak District, Dark Peak

ACCESS *Start from the large car park at the junction with the valley road, just south of the village centre. Served by Manchester-Sheffield trains and Summer Sunday/BH Monday buses from Chesterfield, Hayfield and Castleton. Alternative starts are Barber Booth and Mam Nick car parks.*

A splendid excursion linking the Vale of Edale with the high level march over its southern skyline. For more on Edale, see WALK 14.

S **Leave the car park and head north into the village as far as a bend just before the National Park Visitor Centre.** In front is Champion House, the old vicarage and now a residential youth centre of the diocese of Derby. **Turn left through a gap-stile and giving the house there a wide berth cross to a stile.** Directly left over the railway station are our prime objectives, Mam Tor and Rushup Edge, while ahead is our first goal, the dalehead.

Head away along a couple of fieldsides, and from a tiny stream at the end bear left to a waymark ahead, beneath the farm of Shaw Wood. Cross a stile and straight over the farm drive to another. Now bear left down to the field corner opposite, and from the stile march on

along the bottom of several fields. Ultimately a track forms, becoming enclosed to reach the railway line. Turn left over the bridge and down a hedgerowed lane into Barber Booth. This peaceful hamlet is one of a handful of 'booths', historic settlements found scattered around the Vale of Edale and which together form the parish of Edale.

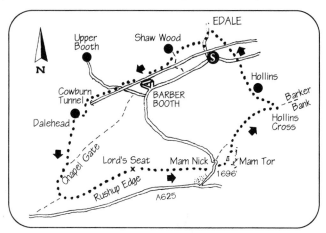

Turn right along the back road through the hamlet, and after a left bend towards the 'main' road, turn sharp right on a rough road passing Edale Methodist church. This was built in 1811 as a Wesleyan Methodist Chapel. **Keep straight on to the lane's demise in the yard of Whitmore Lea Farm. Cross to the gate opposite from where a track rises to bridge the railway again.** Looking left, the line is very shortly to enter the Cowburn Tunnel: completed in 1895, it is 3702 yards long and burrows up to 800ft below the moortop. **Across, turn sharp left on the track parallel to the line. When it swings away, drop down the slope on the left to a wooden footbridge on the river Noe, joining the road beneath the 4-arched railway viaduct.**

Turn right on the road just as far as Barber Booth car park, after which turn left on a farm road. This turns to rise to a fork. At the same time, the unseen railway enters the tunnel: about us are recolonised spoil heaps. At the fork bear left to wind around and up to Dalehead Farm. This typical old sheepfarm was renovated by the National Trust and is now used as a base for volunteer work parties and for groups as a hostel. It features a useful information shelter.

Rise past the front of the house to a stile by a gate, then go left across the field to another. Cross to a further stile then bear right to find one hidden in the corner. Entering the wooded confines of Whitemoor Clough, the stream is quickly crossed and a thin path rises up the other bank. This now makes a concerted climb, thin and very pleasurable, to meet Chapel Gate at an old guidepost. Looking back over the vale, Grindslow Knoll is the most prominent feature of Kinder Scout. Chapel Gate itself is, as its name implies, the old way (a 'gate' being an old road) to Chapel-en-le-Frith.

Dalehead Farm, Edale

Turn right along this old way, virtually at its summit as it swings around the watershed to another guidepost at a junction of ways and old walls. Ahead are sweeping views over Chapel-en-le-Frith, to Cracken Edge and various other features. At the junction Chapel Gate turns right between walls. Our way turns left, a broad path making a long, gentle haul along Rushup Edge to its crest on Lord's Seat. Part-way along, bridleway and path split to opposite sides of the wall, though the bridleway across the wall is actually much less firm than our path. Arrival on Lord's Seat is no major event in itself, except that we now earn views ahead, to Mam Tor and the ridge beyond, and left over the Vale of Edale to the great mass of Kinder.

Descending, the ridge narrows to shapely proportions. Beneath us on the left are countless lumpy mounds, the result of landslips long ago. **The path drops left to meet the road through Mam Nick.** The easiest option (especially if a gale is blowing) drops left to the next bend, where a gate sees a bridleway off, rising very gently around the northern flank of Mam Tor to pick up the ridge path on the descent at the other side. **To take in Mam Tor's crest, turn right over the brow of the road, quickly joining a path on the left and follow its man-made course right up to the waiting Ordnance Survey column (S4230) at 1696ft/517m.**

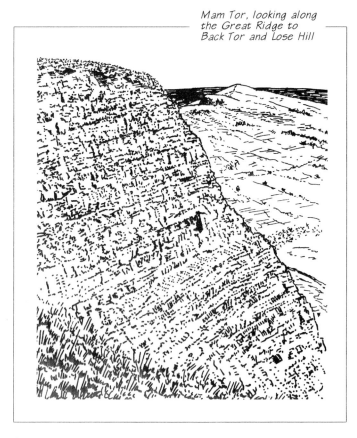

Mam Tor, looking along the Great Ridge to Back Tor and Lose Hill

Mam Tor is commonly known as the 'Shivering Mountain', in deference to the alarmingly unstable face it presents to the Hope Valley. The shaley slopes (sandstone alternating with layers of 'mudstone') have seen numerous landslips (at times of severe weather), and one particularly violent episode was the last straw for the A625 along its flank: the road was abandoned and left to the elements. That gap on the map says it all, though light traffic still has the use of the Winnats Pass to link the Hope Valley with Chapel-en-le-Frith and points west.

Unquestionably a classic Peakland viewpoint, one must nevertheless move a few yards to bring in more intimate valley views to join the likes of Kinder, the ridge to Lose Hill, and the Derwent edges. Visitors stood on its broad grassy summit would do well to remember the lethal drop awaiting from the hill's east face, particularly the tourist wandering casually up from Mam Nick car park. By veering a little to the north we can look down on the very well defined ramparts that once helped defend a possibly 3000 year old, 16 acre Iron Age hillfort on the summit.

A similar path heads away, returning to its natural eroded surface part-way down. The bridleway is absorbed from the left and the path runs along the ridgetop to Hollins Cross. A memorial cairn marks this junction of modern ways overlaying old packhorse routes. The ridge onwards to Back Tor and Lose Hill is tempting, but steps must be retraced or a circuitous way found to return to Edale. **Saving the rest of the ridge for another day (see the companion volume *Central Peak*), turn down the worn bridleway on the left to commence a very quick return. At an early fork a path turns right off the bridleway, descending more steeply to Hollins Farm. Take a stile to its left, joining the farm drive to drop down to bridge the river Noe and up onto the road.**

Cross to a stile opposite and up the fieldside. From a splendid squeezer-stile on the left cross to a railway underpass. A green track rises away, then take another such stile on the left and cross the fields, past a barn to the wooded confines of Grinds Brook. Just ahead, a bridge crosses the stream and the path rises onto the road into Edale village opposite the church. Go right for the centre, left for the car park.

13

RINGING ROGER & JACOB'S LADDER

START *Edale*   *Grid ref. SK 123852*

DISTANCE *8½ miles*

ORDNANCE SURVEY MAPS
1:50,000
Landranger 110 - Sheffield & Huddersfield
1:25,000
Outdoor Leisure 1 - Peak District, Dark Peak

ACCESS *Start from the large car park by the station at the village entrance. Served by Manchester-Sheffield trains and Summer Sunday/BH Monday buses from Hayfield, Chesterfield and Castleton.*
• *ACCESS AREA - see page 8.*

Exploring the southern edges of Kinder Scout, using a classic ascent route and an historic return. For comment on Edale please refer to WALK 14. Map and compass recommended.

S   **Head up the road into the heart of the village, past the *Old Nag's Head* and on beyond a cluster of cottages to the road end. Leave the ensuing rough road by a path signed off to the right, descending to cross a footbridge on Grinds Brook.** This traditional start of the Pennine Way, since replaced by what is to be our return route, has a timeless feel as it leads into the Grindsbrook meadows, regardless of its lost status. Its popularity stems from mere mortals simply wanting to experience the first mile of the big daddy of long distance walks.

Up the other side, the Grindsbrook path runs off to the left, almost entirely flagged throughout its crossing of the pastures. However, leaving Grinds Brook to recover from its fame, our route makes an immediate assault on higher ground. **So, very quickly branch off the**

**Yellow Brick Road and slant up to a stile in the top corner. The path
rises past the tiny Heardman's Plantation to zigzag up the flanks of
the Nab.** Savour impressive views down into the rough fastnesses of
Grinds Brook as it carves a deep defile into Kinder's southern face. **The
path then runs on the heathery ridge.** A branch left cuts more directly
across to gain the path onto Nether Tor at the head of Golden Clough.

**Our described route continues up to mount the frowning rocky spur
of Ringing Roger. Here, amidst temporary fencing to encourage
regeneration of the vegetation, the southern edges path is joined. Go
left, rising steadily towards the greater wall of Nether Tor.** Some
peatier sections of path feature en route. **Grand rock scenery livens
the crossing of Nether Tor before a pull onto Upper Tor.** Fronting
Hartshorn, this is the highest point around and earns views north over
nearby Blackden Edge. The view down into Edale and Grindsbrook
Clough is backed by the seemingly vertical wall of Grindslow Knoll.

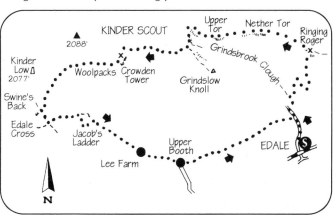

**After a steady descent the path curves above Grindsbrook's upper
reaches, doubling back above lofty pinnacles to ford the stream, a
grand corner. The path doubles back out with super views through
the upper portals of the brook to Grindslow Knoll. Very quickly a
massive cairn is reached after a tiny stream crossing, signifying the
Grindsbrook path's arrival on the plateau at Fox Holes.** Shorter
options here are to descend the initially very rough path into
Grindsbrook, or trace the edge to the beckoning Grindslow Knoll,
passing the prominent boulder known as the Anvil.

The main path bears left across the moor on immediately juicy peat. The alternative edge path to Grindslow Knoll then runs west to regain the edge proper. **The direct path strikes across the moor to quickly gain the forming edge, continuing on in much improved condition to the head of Crowden Clough, with the buttresses of Crowden Tower just beyond.** Gain its rocky crest to admire the view down into the clough from this airy vantage point.

Grindslow Knoll from Upper Tor

The main path (there are several variants) continues west across the moor into the heart of the remarkable Woolpacks: prepare to spend some time exploring. Any number of formations can be located and named in this absorbing wonderland also known as Whipsnade. **At the far end is the major outcrop known as the Pagoda.** Illustrated on page 56, it overlooks the valley and can be scaled with ease. Here we are looking down on Edale Head, Jacob's Ladder and Youngate packhorse bridge at its foot. At the 'moor' side of our immediate rocks, the shapely stones of Pym Chair are prominent.

Resume along the edge path, passing the highly individual tor of Noe Stool. Continue round with the remains of a wall to drop down to meet the Pennine Way at a cairn beneath Swine's Back. This rebuilt path drops down to meet the Hayfield-Edale track. Turn left, quickly beginning a steep descent of Jacob's Ladder, an historic route restored in 1987. Note that this is the direct footpath, and an alternative, easier graded bridleway zigzags on the right.

The ways re-unite at the bottom to cross Youngate Bridge. This old packhorse bridge occupies a delightful spot where the waters of the Cloughs tumble beneath. Head away on the broad path along to Lee Farm. Here the National Trust have provided an information shelter. Continue along the farm road to Upper Booth. This attractive hamlet features a postbox within the farmyard, and a camping barn.

Opposite the phone box turn up into the farmyard, bearing right before the main house and up a rough lane. Branch right off this as indicated for Edale, rising up a rough walled lane. Emerging into the fields the path slants up to a brow at Broadlee-bank. From this modest brow there are grand views over the vale, all the way down to the shapely peak of Lose Hill. From this point it is downhill to Edale, slanting through the pastures on a largely flagged path. The final stage sees it turn down to the right, becoming enclosed by foliage to emerge into the village rather handily opposite the *Old Nag's Head*.

*Pym Chair,
Kinder Scout*

14

JAGGERS CLOUGH

START *Edale*　　　　*Grid ref. SK 123852*

DISTANCE *7 miles*

ORDNANCE SURVEY MAPS
1:50,000
Landranger 110 - Sheffield & Huddersfield
1:25,000
Outdoor Leisure 1 - Peak District, Dark Peak

ACCESS *Start from the large car park at the junction with the valley road, just south of the village centre. Served by Manchester-Sheffield trains and Summer Sunday/BH Monday buses from Hayfield, Chesterfield and Castleton. • ACCESS AREA - see page 8.*

Much moorland variety as trods along the base and upper edges of Kinder Scout are linked by the loveliest of its many deep cloughs. If you're the one member of your walking club that buys guidebooks, please don't recommend this walk, and certainly don't bring them. Let's keep it a reasonable secret: Jaggers Clough is too good - and in the long term too fragile - for large groups. Map and compass strongly recommended.

🅢　Edale is a near legendary place, known only to local ramblers until the Pennine Way was deemed to begin its lumbering journey to the Scottish border from here. Despite this fame, one could be forgiven for thinking it has had no effect on the place: stand in the centre and there are the *Old Nag's Head* inn, school, Post office/shop, a phone box and a few hugely attractive cottages. In truth, little *has* changed, and for the tourist there is little to do but gawp for five minutes then get on your way. For walkers however, Edale will always be the major jumping off point for untold excursions onto Kinder Scout: the affinity between the two is in the Matterhorn/Zermatt mould.

The tall spired church of the Holy and Undivided Trinity looks down upon the scene, which working back down the road also features a National Park Visitor Centre/Mountain Rescue Post, the *Rambler Inn*, (formerly the *Church Inn*) a tiny cafe, railway station and toilets. Unseen by most Edale visitors is a tiny old packhorse bridge, spanning Grinds Brook just down past the *Old Nag's Head*.

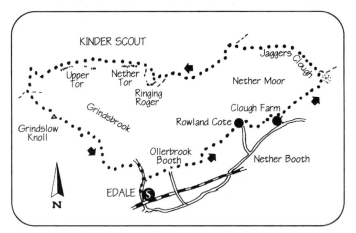

From the car park head up the road towards the village centre. After the visitor centre, however, take a short-lived walled way on the right opposite Church Cottage. Note a 1678 datestone in the roadside wall here. **The little path descends past the campsite to a bridge on Grinds Brook, then rises away, first as a broad path, then a track to the hamlet of Ollerbrook Booth.** This proves to be an interesting settlement featuring some attractive cottages. **Pass straight through, remaining on the broad track out the other side. Keep on below the farm of Cotefield, now on a broad path.**

After two further fields, take an easily missed branch up to the left (not as per map). This climbs the fence-side then slants across to the top of the wooded grounds of a house on the right. Continue above here on a grand path through gorse and scrub. Lose Hill and Back Tor look particularly fine across the valley, with Win Hill ahead linked to our eastern end of Kinder. **The path runs on through several fields to Rowland Cote.** Here stands the Edale youth hostel, a busy activity centre based in a big house in a grand setting.

Go right up to the house and along the front: at the end the path drops to a footbridge on Lady Booth Brook. From the stile we enter Open Country of the National Trust's Nether Moor. The path runs on above the intake wall, a smashing tramp as it passes above Clough Farm. Ahead are views to Derwent Edge on the skyline. The path runs on to merge into a broad track, rising to a brow then slanting back into Jaggers Clough. Ahead, the true summit of Win Hill is revealed. Turning this corner the sudden prospect of the clough and Kinder's lesser known eastern flank is revealed with Crookstone Knoll on the skyline. At the hairpin by the stream, leave the track and turn upstream (opposite bank) on a contrastingly slender path.

The clough takes its name from packhorse times, for a jagger was the 'master' of the train of pack mules, and the track that brought us into the clough is an old trading route linking Edale with the Woodlands Valley and beyond. Our route remains well defined throughout the course of the clough, climbing gently in the narrow but not entirely cramped confines, just us and the stream. This is a magical section.

A tight section sees the path briefly share the stream bed before opening out beneath the upper section. The going steepens as the path clambers up and through tumbling stones, becoming rougher as it climbs onto a path contouring across the clough. Don't leave here but continue up, within fifty yards finding a better path crossing the clough. Go left with this path, climbing a little before contouring round the moor. It soon rises to meet a broader path. Go left on this to resume the contour, swinging round onto the southern face and traversing high above Ollerbrook Clough, with the youth hostel prominent. The vale is outspread with the Mam Tor ridge beyond, and the limestone scars of the Winnats very distinct over Hollins Cross.

The way remains clear as it rises to a better defined edge (Rowland Cote Moor), then on with Ringing Roger thrusting prominently out ahead. A path merges in from the left, then as one slants down, we work up to the right. Note that an easy finish is the path down to the plateau under Ringing Roger, crossing right to gain the main path descending to the Grindsbrook meadows.

Keep on to the edge above the rocks of Ringing Roger before doubling back around a fenced enclosure, rising steadily towards the greater wall of Nether Tor. Some peatier sections of path feature in these parts. Our path crosses the top of Nether Tor with some grand rocks

in attendance, before a pull onto Upper Tor. This is the highest point around and earns views north over nearby Blackden Edge. The view down into Edale and Grindsbrook Clough is backed by the seemingly vertical wall of Grindslow Knoll (see illustration on page 64).

After a steady descent the path curves round above Grindsbrook's upper reaches, doubling back above lofty pinnacles to ford the stream, a grand corner. The path doubles back out with super views through the upper portals of the brook to Grindslow Knoll. Very quickly a massive cairn is reached after a tiny stream crossing, signifying the Grindsbrook path's arrival on the plateau at Fox Holes. Though one could simply descend the initially very rough path into the clough to follow Grinds Brook down to the village, better to remain on the edge to the beckoning Grindslow Knoll. En route a prominent boulder known as the Anvil is passed.

The well defined top of Grindslow Knoll affords good views all round, and offers a quick and easy descent. **Head south-east from the cairn towards Edale, at once picking up a clear path that drops down through the heather. Beyond a cairn fashioned from an old wall it drops more gently, around the head of a minor clough and then starts to wind down to the right, well worn. Part hollowed, it reaches a stile into the pastures (end of Open Country). Curve down here to meet the Pennine Way route at a stile on the right. Continue straight down however to quickly become enclosed by foliage to emerge into the village centre rather handily opposite the** *Old Nag's Head.*

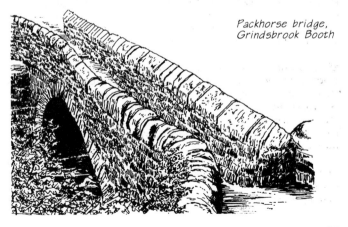

Packhorse bridge, Grindsbrook Booth

15

HOPE CROSS

START *Woodlands Valley*   *Grid ref. SK 164878*

DISTANCE *3½ miles*

ORDNANCE SURVEY MAPS
1:50,000
Landranger 110 - Sheffield & Huddersfield
1:25,000
Outdoor Leisure 1 - Peak District, Dark Peak

ACCESS *Start from Severn-Trent Water's Ladybower Reservoir park-*
ing area (currently signed only as a public footpath) at the head of the
western arm of the reservoir, half a mile off the A57 2 miles west of
Ashopton Viaduct. Alternatively, start from a roadside parking area
50 yards south of Hagg Farm Centre, half a mile further north - GR
162885) and pick up the route via Haggwater Bridge. Summer
Sunday/BH Monday buses from Manchester, Rochdale, Sheffield and
Matlock all use the Snake Pass between Glossop and Ladybower.

A very easy walk: a quick up and down sandwiched between a
waterside walk and a high level ridge embracing superb views.

❺ **Leave the car park by crossing the bridge over the Ashop and
heading off along the forest road. Almost at once however is a
branch right. Turn up this, passing a sign to the Roman road sending
a narrow path climbing into the trees, and remain on the broad track.
This soon rises to a stile and a gate to meet another track on a hairpin
bend. Go left, winding up through the trees and emerging at a gate
out onto rougher pasture.**

Remain on the track alongside the plantation. Views quickly unfold
as we approach the ridge-top, with Win Hill and Lose Hill ahead,
framing Bradwell Moor. Left of Win Hill is Stanage Edge, a glimpse of

Ladybower Reservoir and the twin tors of Crook Hill. **Yards further we gain the brow at a junction.** Beyond Lose Hill are Back Tor, Mam Tor, the Vale of Edale and the eastern edge of Kinder Scout with Crookstone Knoll prominent: a cracking moment - and with most of the hard work already accomplished.

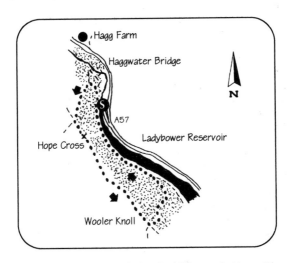

Go left, descending to a gate behind which stands Hope Cross. This old waymarker survives from the packhorse days when it marked an important crossroads. It is dated 1737 and bears the names of Hope, Edale, Glossop and Shefield (sic). It originally stood a little higher up the ridge, at the junction of tracks we have just left. The ridge track we are now following goes much further back, for it is also part of the Roman road linking forts at MELANDRA, near Glossop and NAVIO, near Brough in the Hope Valley just below us. From here the Vale of Edale is magnificently laid out, cosily enclosed by the Mam Tor ridge and the Kinder massif.

Resume along the broad track, bearing away from the trees between long crumbled walls. Emerging into open country at a stile and gate, forsake the main track and take a clear broad way slanting up to the left (this is the bridleway the map depicts as being further along). This soon slants up as a more inviting green way to regain the broad ridge, again with the trees clinging to the watershed.

Ultimately rising all the way to the summit of Win Hill, we follow the ridge just as far as a crossroads with a cross-ridge footpath at Wooler Knoll. This is confirmed by the presence of an old cross-wall, the branching off the ridge of the trees, and also the beginnings of heather moorland ahead on the rising path to Win Hill. Those with time and energy might choose to reach the summit: certainly it is worth the modest effort (it is visited from Hope in the companion volume, *Central Peak*).

Our more modest jaunt turns left here, abandoning the ridge at a stile into the trees. A broad track descends away, swinging left then continuing more firmly down to a T-junction. While the obvious way is to swing left again to drop down to the forest road along the shore of Ladybower Reservoir, the true public footpath is somewhat obscure but worth finding. Simply continue straight down at this crossroads, the unconvincing way initially hampered and dubious but within 100 yards, passing through an old wall, the path will be seen. At once it becomes a quality path, slanting left and descending unfailingly and far more pleasantly to the forest road.

Now simply turn left along the hard forest road, for a good mile, enjoying views over this upper western arm of the reservoir and further up the valley, to soon return to the bridge and thus the finish.

Hope Cross, looking to Lose Hill, Back Tor & Mam Tor

16

LOCKERBROOK RIDGE

START *Ladybower Reservoir*   *Grid ref. SK 172892*

DISTANCE *5 miles*

ORDNANCE SURVEY MAPS
1:50,000
Landranger 110 - Sheffield & Huddersfield
1:25,000
Outdoor Leisure 1 - Peak District, Dark Peak

ACCESS *Start from the Fairholmes visitor centre car park at the head of Ladybower Reservoir in the Upper Derwent Valley. This is the main car park for the upper dale, 2 miles off the A57. Served by Sheffield-Castleton buses (infrequent) and by numerous seasonal services, the most regular being from Sheffield.*

⑤ Fairholmes is focal point for visitors to the Upper Derwent Valley. Here is a small visitor centre (run by Severn-Trent Water and the National Park), refreshment kiosk, toilets, cycle hire and ranger base.

Leave the car park by the road exit onto the valley road, and straight across a 'concession footpath' is signed to Lockerbrook. This rises through the trees, ignoring a couple of branches right for Derwent Reservoir: the second of these leaves at a broad water drain. The path climbs to emerge onto a hard forest road. Go left up through the hairpin then take a signed path (forest walk) on the left. This soon rises more gently and pleasantly to another fork, keeping right up a few steps. The path passes through an old wall then swings left to a stile out of the plantation.

Lockerbrook Farm appears just over to the left. The main path heads directly away from the stile, through new plantings to a stile onto a broad track. Turn left to Lockerbrook. This isolated house occupies a grand position overlooking Ladybower Reservoir far down in the valley. **Continue away on its drive, within a couple of minutes arriving at a crossroads.** Rapidly, a superb panorama spreads out in front. The first sighting is of Mam Tor, quickly joined by its ridge to Lose Hill and the eastern bulk of Kinder Scout.

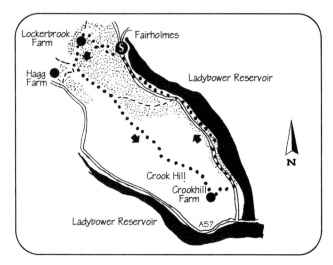

Our way is left, along the broad ridge-top outside the plantation. Throughout this stage the views to the right are superb. **At a junction with a short-cut to Bridge End car park keep straight on the edge of the wood, losing both the views and the open pasture. Rising away, as the trees swing left advance to a stile/gate in the wall ahead. A fainter path runs on through pleasant pasture, a fine stroll to the walk's summit on Bridge-end Pasture overlooking Crook Hill.** The view revealed from this 1279ft/390m brow is a gem. Pride of place goes to the twin peaks of Crook Hill, a fine pair of shaggy terriers. There is a glimpse of Ladybower Reservoir down to the left, while beyond, Stanage Edge leads the eye over further eastern scarps.

Resuming, the way drops to a bridle-gate and then as a thin trod down a field to a corner gate. Heading away, the track swings left away from Crook Hill and becomes clearer at an old ditch. It then runs on to approach Crookhill Farm. Ahead, the Ashopton Viaduct is in view. **While the bridleway goes through the yard to meet the**

farm drive, the National Trust has created a concession path avoiding the farmyard. This is indicated at a gate on the left, slanting down the field to the left of the farm buildings. From the gate join the drive and turn down to meet the Upper Derwent Valley road.

Turn left on the footway for five minutes as far as Hurst Clough car park, then take the chance of a reservoir shore path by dropping down through the grassy picnic area. Immediately passing between aqueduct pipes, head up-dale on a good path through the trees. This emerges into the open just beneath a 1914-18 war memorial on the road above. Now we have good views over the reservoir to Derwent Edge, with the tor known as the Salt Cellar prominent.

Beyond the memorial, road and path arrive at Bridge End car park. Across the dale from here stood Derwent village. Principal feature of this tight-knit community was Derwent Hall. Dating from 1672, it was a shooting lodge of the Duke of Norfolk, and finished its days as a youth hostel (1927-43). Much of the remains of the demolished village can still be discerned at times of low water, and leaflets offering further and fascinating information can be obtained locally.

From Bridge End a concession path resumes up-dale, largely on a firm surface. The path passes the start of the aqueduct over the reservoir, built to link the Derwent dam directly to the treatment works. The path rejoins the road at the Derwent Overlook car park, just short of the start.

Winter on Crook Hill

17

BLACKDEN BROOK & BLACKDEN EDGE

START *Woodlands Valley*   *Grid ref. SK 130895*

DISTANCE *6½ miles*

ORDNANCE SURVEY MAPS
1:50,000
Landranger 110 - Sheffield & Huddersfield
1:25,000
Outdoor Leisure 1 - Peak District, Dark Peak

ACCESS *Start from the A57 beneath Blackden View Farm: there is a large lay-by here equidistant from the Snake Pass Inn and Alport Bridge. Summer Sunday/BH Monday buses from Manchester, Rochdale, Sheffield and Matlock all use the Snake Pass between Glossop and Ladybower.* • *ACCESS AREA - see page 8.*

A rewarding excursion into lesser known parts of Kinder Scout. The plateau is gained via a steep-walled clough, with a fine walk on the tops to the classic viewpoint of Crookstone Knoll. Map and compass strongly recommended.

ⓢ **From the lay-by a stile sends a path down the field to a bridge on the river Ashop. The path climbs the slope behind to a ladder-stile into Open Country, then rises right to follow the wall towards the deep folds of Blackden Brook. It contours round to enter the confines of the clough, and soon runs alongside the stream before crossing it.**

The clear path advances up the clough, a superb walk through charming surrounds. High to the left is Blackden Edge, which we shall be striding before long. Occasional trees and a re-crossing at a particularly sinuous section add interest and colour as the winding clough penetrates the hills. A particularly fine moment is the climb above an impasse caused by a notable little waterfall: watch for one or two sections of landslip on the path.

Only in the latter stages does real uphill work begin, as the ground steepens and the path on occasions merges with the stream bed. At the start of this rougher section note a lovely long waterslide opposite. In the final section successive branches strike up to the left, both offering more serious scrambling opportunities out of the clough. **The recommended route keeps faith with the main stream, ultimately offering very mild scrambling before sudden emergence onto the well defined Blackden Edge.**

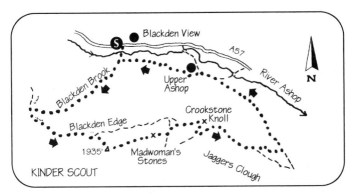

This is a moment to savour as the moor stretches away and far-reaching views are revealed. **Turn left along the edge to commence a grand mile, keeping to the lower path for the finest atmosphere. Beyond the heads of the side cloughs the path runs on to occasional rock outcrops and boulders.** Views back up the Woodlands Valley and across to the great sprawl of Bleaklow are matched by more intimate ones down to the foot of Blackden Brook. **At a notable group of rocks the white painted Ordnance Survey column at 1935ft/590m on the plateau should appear ahead.**

Though one can retain the edge path all the way round to Crookstone Knoll (and indeed should in poor conditions) this offers a finer route. Strike out over easy heather moor for just a few minutes to reach the OS column (S4231), possibly on a thin trod. Here we are greeted by a fine prospect south into the heart of the Peak, but perhaps most interesting is the appearance of Grindslow Knoll across the plateau, with such Kinder landmarks as Swine's Back, the Pagoda (Woolpacks) and Hartshorn also featuring. The Mam Tor ridge also slots in, though it will be better seen over the ensuing mile.

Leave by heading just north of east on one of several ways, here encountering the walk's only true peaty moments. The rocks of Madwoman's Stones should be sighted further along, and the way leads there, probably via a prominent boss of rock that proves to be a pair. Two minutes further the cluster of Madwoman's Stones is reached. Though not of great proportions or shape, they are nevertheless a notable landmark on this part of Kinder.

On Crookstone Knoll, looking to Win Hill and Derwent Edge

Due east again, Crookstone Knoll should be clear. A path heads that way, quickly being halted at rock tables marking a notable path junction. By now, Back Tor's fine profile is tagged onto Lose Hill. **Take the branch sharp left, after fifty yards forking right and remaining on this good path which swings right to drop down and run on an improving little edge to Crookstone Knoll.**

This is effectively the eastern outpost of Kinder's mighty plateau, and certainly when stood upon the little rocks of this promontory, it feels the part. The view stretches from the Mam Tor ridge in the south, round by Stanage Edge and the Derwent Valley to the Derwent Edges above Ladybower Reservoir, then the Alport and Woodlands Valleys and finally Blackden Edge and Fairbrook Naze.

Resume by doubling back to the right on the main path, with Mam Tor straight ahead. Within a couple of minutes leave this by doubling back again, this time sharply left on a broad path slanting down beneath some rocks. This clear path winds down the moor past a more substantial cliff face and down to a stile and gate. The Mam Tor ridge continues to be well arrayed during this stage. **Here the moor proper is left for a lush green track though grassy pasture. At a couple of landmark trees on Crookstone Hill a branch path left is our way, dropping down to meet a broad track on the edge of Open Country.**

Don't take the gate but remain in Open Country by going left on the track, rising briefly and crossing Blackley Clough before a second brow precedes a steady descent. The track drops to meet a drive at a hairpin. Keep left here towards the lone house of Upper Ashop. Note that a branch right just before the house sends a track down onto the road at Alport Bridge for a quicker road finish.

The Great Ridge from Crookstone Hill,
featuring Back Tor and Mam Tor

Don't enter the house's confines but turn left over a stream and up with the intake wall, rising briefly then running on above the wall. Straight across the main valley is Alport Dale, with the Castles and Tower well seen (see WALK 19). **Crossing over a track our trod contours on (don't lose height with the wall), encountering two cloughs.** The second is crossed above an example of the National Trust's woodland conservation scheme: stiles see us across the temporary fencing that excludes foraging sheep. **The wall returns to lead very quickly back to the Open Country stile, finishing as we started with the bridge on the Ashop.**

18

ASHOP CLOUGH & ASHOP EDGE

START Woodlands Valley   Grid ref. SK 112905

DISTANCE 8¼ miles

ORDNANCE SURVEY MAPS
1:50,000
Landranger 110 - Sheffield & Huddersfield
1:25,000
Outdoor Leisure 1 - Peak District, Dark Peak

ACCESS Start from the A57 by the Snake Pass Inn. Its own car park is strictly for patrons, but there are some good verges just down from the pub. As these quickly fill up at weekends, it may be necessary to use the Birchin Clough car park half a mile up the pass. From here gain the route by using the Lady Clough Forest Trail immediately opposite the car park. Summer Sunday/BH Monday buses from Manchester, Rochdale, Sheffield and Matlock all use the Snake Pass between Glossop and Ladybower. • ACCESS AREA - see page 8.

Whilst tradition suggests ascents be steep and quick and returns gentle and drawn out, this route is described in the manner I found more satisfying, beginning with a long stroll up Ashop Clough. There are of course benefits the other way, and as route description is largely incidental to this walk one could easily take the clockwise option. Ideally, come back another day, another season and reverse the route! Map and compass strongly recommended

S The Snake Pass was opened as a turnpike road in 1821, one of its promoters being the Duke of Devonshire. This was the last of the great turnpikes. The pub was a tollhouse until 1870, and a posting house where horses were changed after the rigours of the climb. The Snake derives from a feature on the coat of arms of the Devonshires.

From the *Snake Pass Inn* **head up the road on the useful footway. Just after the trees on the left start, a stile sends a path down through them to meet the river Ashop.** The scene here is reminiscent of a Scottish glen. **Turn upstream, quickly passing a stile (where the Lady Clough path comes in) and over a footbridge. Ahead the valley of Ashop Clough is outspread, with moorland to one side and forest on the other: soon all will be strictly moorland. Part-way on, a stile takes the main path into the trees, and a good path runs on to a stile at the end of the plantation.** Here the Open Country of the National Trust's Ashop Moor is entered.

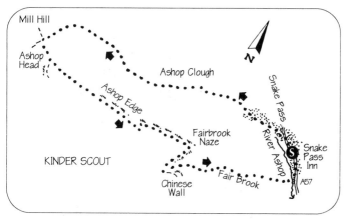

Immediately across the main brook, Urchin Clough tumbles excitedly down the moor. **Our superb path runs on updale and further instructions for the ascent of Ashop Clough are largely superfluous, there being only one path all the way to the top.** En route we quickly encounter a tumbling side-stream (Nether Gate Clough), with the first sighting of the edges of our return route towering high above: very quickly the full length slides into view. It is surprising how little effort is needed to actually attain that height, for our route is very gradual indeed.

A dodgy landslip section is quickly traversed before slanting down towards the brook. Passing above a ruinous hut a lesser path comes in at a plank bridge. The layout changes as the valley broadens and the path suffers some peaty spells. All the while the craggy escarp-ment towers above. At an attractive confluence of twin streams our

path keeps left, and continues the gentle rise until we return to a deeper, now tiny ravine. The path has a spell virtually up the brook before rising above its bank to quickly attain the summit of the Snake Path at Ashop Head. This is marked by an attractive modern guidepost, and here our route meets the Pennine Way.

The Boxing Glove Rocks, Ashop Edge

Turn left to enjoy a short clamber up the big end on a stone pitched path onto the Kinder plateau: a fine moment indeed! While the main path bears right to follow the western edge, rise instead gently left to the nearest group of rocks. Here a clearer path is met contouring round from the western edge, and so begins the crossing of Ashop Edge. The path remains clear throughout, the first half-mile being better spent savouring the broad views over the Woodlands Valley to Bleaklow until more immediate interest is found. This comes with the first cluster of rocks on the edge, very soon after which the Boxing Glove Rocks are a very distinguishable feature.

The path runs on above crags and boulders of varying grandeur, but every step is a grand one. Before too long we find ourselves approaching the corner known as Fairbrook Naze. Here the path has a crisis of identity as a branch swings inland to cut the corner. Remain on the edge and from the end look down on our descent route: indeed, one could descend from the Naze (or 'nose') itself. Better to continue along to the right above the last few outcrops to the deep indentation that is the head of Fair Brook.

Only at the crossing point does the descent path set off. Thin but clear, it clambers down the rocky way in close company with the infant brook. This remains so for several hundred feet with the walls above increasing in grandeur. As the gradient eases the path swings away from the brook and enjoys a steadier drop, affording more time to appraise the edges above. Up to the right is the bold scarp of the Chinese Wall.

The path in its lower stages is drawn back in towards the brook as the walls steepen again. The highlight comes at a confluence of tumbling streams amidst a few trees, while the Chinese Wall and Fairbrook Naze look down from on high. A short level section draws things to a close as a wall and National Trust sign are reached. The path winds up left to run on to a footbridge over the river Ashop. A path then climbs through the tiny plantation to a stile onto the road, with the pub just two minutes up to the left.

The Snake Pass Inn

19

ALPORT DALE

START *Woodlands Valley*   *Grid ref. SK 109914*

DISTANCE *9 miles*

ORDNANCE SURVEY MAPS
1:50,000
Landranger 110 - Sheffield & Huddersfield
1:25,000
Outdoor Leisure 1 - Peak District, Dark Peak

ACCESS *Start from Birchin Clough car park in Snake Woodlands, half a mile west of the Snake Pass Inn. Summer Sunday/BH Monday buses from Manchester, Rochdale, Sheffield and Matlock all use the Snake Pass.* • *ACCESS AREA - see page 8.*

A largely straightforward walk with a mix of moorland and valley: one steep rougher section only, and pathless moorland at the end. Map and compass strongly recommended. For a shorter, easier walk Alport Castles can be visited from Alport Bridge, returning the same way: this can be enjoyed during 'closed' spells, as it is on a public footpath.

❺ **From the car park head down the road's grassy verge, and within a couple of minutes a footpath is signed off to the left.** Opinions differ as to whether this is the course of the Roman road linking forts at MELANDRA, near Glossop and NAVIO, near Brough in the Hope Valley. **Rising through the trees the path soon begins an undulating course.** Up above, the rocky Dinas Sitch Tor is virtually hidden by foliage.

Emerging from the trees to enter the Open Country of the National Trust's Alport Moor, the path slants up the pasture. Over to the right, the northern edges of Kinder form an unbroken wall, with the Chinese Wall and Fairbrook Naze featuring prominently. **At a fork take the**

level branch, passing above the trees to reach a brow and a 1928 guidepost. Ahead is the edge of Cowms Rocks. The path descends steeply to cross Oyster Clough and up the wall-side opposite.

The path passes through a couple of stiles; one by a recently restored sheepfold, another at a stream crossing. Leaving rougher terrain the path becomes fainter as it curves around a large pasture. It runs around to be joined by a wall from the right. At this point there is brief uncovered evidence of stone flags that once formed this historic path. Though much more recent than Roman, they confirm the importance of this route over a longer period, most notably the packhorse era.

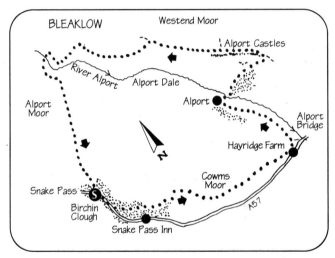

Continue along the wall-side on an improving green path beneath Cowms Moor. This NT land is less of a moor than the following enclosure! The way slants down, remaining with the wall, and down again to become enclosed just short of Hayridge Farm. Approaching the buildings the path is diverted left across to a ladder-stile, then on again to meet the Alport hamlet road just above the farm. Go left on this firm drive for a good mile. There is a 'Scottish glen' feel to this approach, which presents fine views of Alport Castles up to the right as we penetrate the foot of this side valley. Between Alport hamlet and Glethering Clough further updale there is no access, but our route up onto the edge is in any case an integral part of the walk.

The drive ends at the hamlet. Alport is the setting, each July, for a 'Love Feast', a religious service with 18th century origins. Less endearing are forestry plans to devastate the valley with a heavy duty access road: a cause of much upset, needless to say. Happily the hamlet's two residences are both in occupation.

While the public footpath goes through the hamlet then doubles back outside the wall to the right, a concessionary path avoids intruding by taking a couple of stiles on the right, then down to meet the public footpath just above the stream. Turn downstream from the ford to find a footbridge on the river Alport. Across, a path slants left up to the plantation corner, then heads up through colourful country outside the trees.

When the trees end the path forges on upwards in the company of an old wall, a grand path through grand surrounds. As the going eases the cliffs are better glimpsed up to the left, but the path swings right, rising to a stile at a wall-corner. Rising briefly with the wall it then crosses it to continue up with it. As the wall parts company at a little gateway, Open Country is finally entered. The grassy path rises gently left for two minutes onto the skyline edge, with Alport Castles visible just ahead.

This is a fine moment as ahead the long skyline of the Derwent edges appears beyond the unseen Derwent Valley. Just beneath us though, Alport Castles' pride and joy, the detached Tower, slots in between a knoll and the main edge. **Go left along the edge path, quickly reaching the most dramatic section immediately above the Tower.**

This is a place to linger and savour the situation, though lively young 'uns should not be let too near the edge. The remarkable Tower has been left isolated since an awesome landslip long ago, and is now a proud sentinel and established landmark of Alport Dale. Up-dale is a long, high Bleaklow skyline: in good visibility the tip of the Holme Moss mast pricks out above the Bleaklow Stones-Grinah Stones saddle.

Resume along the edge, the path now shadowing a wall. When this turns away, keep straight on the edge path. It runs past but avoids peaty ground and encounters twin-like minor stream crossings. After the second the main path strikes off up the moor, bound for a white Ordnance Survey column on the broad ridge. Our route

swings left here, remaining on the peaty margin on a slimmer path. Little more than a sheeptrod it faithfully leads around above the steep slope.

On at least two occasions there are glimpses back to the Tower, not easily discerned without the right lighting. The uniform slopes of Alport Dale entirely dominate thoughts now. Note also regular evidence of the trees that once survived up here, in the form of old stumps preserved in the peat.

The Tower, Alport Castles

The trod remains clear all the way round to the pronounced indent of Glethering Clough. Here, with good timing, the slopes below become access land, so beyond the clough slant gently down to join a contouring sheeptrod. This has broadened to accommodate walkers, so resume along it. This stage enjoys the real atmosphere of this infrequently explored valley. Opposite, Nether Reddale Clough falls dramatically to the valley floor, in a series of waterfalls from top to bottom.

The next clough on our side is Miry Clough, with a forlorn tree standing proud, and ahead more glorious country penetrating deeper into Bleaklow's flanks. Whilst it is possible to continue all the way up to its beginnings and thence join the Pennine Way coming down from Bleaklow, our way now chooses to turn for home.

Note that there are few practical places to cross the valley, this being already quite obvious on surveying the steep and often craggy slopes near the stream. Immediately after Miry Clough however we are very near the stream, at its most accessible. Turn down the slope, doubling back to the point where Miry Clough enters the Alport. Some useful stones aid the fording of the main stream, though if in spate it would be easier to go a further mile upstream.

Though the slopes opposite appear intimidating, they are less steep than imagined and the pull of a mere 300 or so feet is quickly accomplished. It is split into two clear sections by a small shelf beneath the few rocks of the upper half. At the top go left on another well defined edge, a trod forged by the sheep leading back around the twin heads of the insignificant Upper Reddale Clough and around to Nether Reddale Clough. There is one unexpected final glimpse of the Tower during this stage.

The faint trod swings in with this deep indent, and forges on to its very head. Keep left with the main stream's grassy banks as it straggles through peat groughs at the very top. Look back over Bleaklow and the Grinah Stones before a sudden deposit onto contrastingly open rough, grassy moor. Best advice is to traverse this final, brief section of pathless moorland with a compass fixed in a south-westerly direction. An imperceptible rise to a brow sees the forming Birchin Clough over to the left. Keep on, slowly dropping southwards a little on the brow. The long line of Kinder Scout ahead is peaked by the knob of Fairbrook Naze. Over to the right, traffic can be seen on the summit of the Snake Pass.

Rougher ground is encountered just before a reasonably clear path should be met. Bear left on it, now heading south across a tongue of moorland with slopes falling away to each side. This improving path runs down to a dramatic stance high above the Woodlands Valley, thence reaching a bird's-eye viewpoint of the car park. A short, steep descent culminates in leaving Open Country by a path through the trees directly to the car park.

GRINAH STONES

START *Derwent Valley*   *Grid ref. SK 167938*

DISTANCE *10 miles*

ORDNANCE SURVEY MAPS
1:50,000
Landranger 110 - Sheffield & Huddersfield
1:25,000
Outdoor Leisure 1 - Peak District, Dark Peak

ACCESS *Start from the King's Tree parking area at the Upper Derwent Valley road end. On Summer weekends/BH Mondays the road is closed, but is accessible by a regular bus service that operates from Fairholmes visitor centre. • ACCESS AREA - see page 8.*

A breezy moorland ramble on the Bleaklow massif, centred on a magnetic natural landmark: broad ridges are linked by deep, characterful cloughs. Map & compass strongly recommended.

S The Upper Derwent Valley is a long cul-de-sac for motorists but an embracing gateway to the moors for walkers. It was first dammed to create Howden Reservoir (1912) and Derwent Reservoir (1916). A railway was built from Bamford to transport men and materials to the Howden dam, and the present road follows much of its course. It was the addition of Ladybower, completed in 1945, however, which caused most grief, for this necessitated the drowning of two villages, Ashopton and Derwent.

Without doubt the valley is best known for the remarkable story of the Dambusters, of which a mere mention has one humming the celebrated march. It was the wartime setting of practice runs by the RAF in preparation for attacking the Ruhr dams in Germany with the celebrated 'bouncing bombs'.

From the parking area head along the broad track continuing from the road end. However, as soon as it crosses inflowing Linch Clough, turn off left, unconvincingly through the trees. This little corner of woodland leads to a gateway in a wall and immediate entry into contrastingly Open Country. A good path sets off up the inviting **Linch Clough.** This opening stage is sheer delight as the deep walled clough is penetrated.

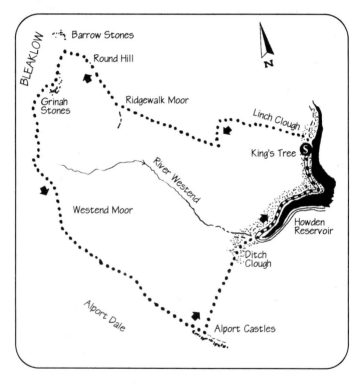

Quite early the green path crosses the stream, and leads with false hopes up the other bank. However, almost at once it forsakes the clough and doubles back up the flank. So, resisting its charms, do not cross the stream with it but forge on the right (north) bank. Sheeptrods soon form and a surprisingly easy and hugely enjoyable section ensues.

This course is charted for some time, a little above the stream but increasingly sharing its cramped confines and featuring several re-crossings. The outside world, and even the rolling moors just above, seem a world away. **Beyond some minor rocky walls and some delectable little waterfalls and waterslides, the clough opens out slightly. After a dead tree a small survivor is met at a bend and a minor confluence. Here strike west-south-west with the tiny inflowing stream. This quickly fades but points a grassy strip up onto open heather moor.**

The green way continues for a couple of minutes to lead unfailingly to the broad, hollowed course of the abandoned drain of Black Dike. Looking back, enjoy a long distance view down the eastern edges and deeper into the heart of the Peak. Westwards, the northern edges of Kinder just break the skyline.

Turn right on this equally inviting way up the broad moorland ridge. It leads to a drain junction at some reedy pools on a knoll. The main arm seems to go left, dropping away, but our path simply forges along the broad Ridgewalk Moor. It crosses the reedy drain in front and passes to the left of a vast, marshy tract, then a true drain returns and our path happily plies on alongside it. Up ahead, the Grinah Stones dominate the skyline, with Bleaklow Stones set back to the left and Round Hill's few boulders to the right, nearest.

The drain ends for good at a peaty channel crossing the ridge. Here a path branches left to the unseen head of a bulldozed shooters' track: this is perhaps better not seen, as it certainly ruins the feeling of being a long way from civilisation. Incidentally a path runs from its turning circle more directly past a cairn and marked by stakes, bound for the Grinah Stones, crossing the head of Grinah Grain. **On the broad ridge, however, the wet path continues. During this stage a fork sends a left branch again striking out for the Grinah Stones. Far better to take the right branch, running on to quickly gain firmer ground and rise pleasantly up onto Round Hill.**

This attractive knoll is marked by a crumbling stone shelter. The outstanding view stretches from the Grinah Stones through a southern arc to Emley Moor mast: two endless skylines on display are Kinder's northern edges and also the Derwent edges. **From here strike inland to the nearby rocks on the skyline. A clear path runs to these southerly outliers of the Barrow Stones. A further path then contin-**

ues left along the little edge to the patiently waiting **Grinah Stones.**
These are by far the finest rocks in the vicinity, indeed usurping those
on Bleaklow Stones itself. Allow sufficient time to explore these grand
stones, a better lunch halt would be hard to imagine.

At the Grinah Stones, looking to Bleaklow Stones

**Leave by going west to the edge of the rocks, then slant down to the
prominent Deep Grain just beneath. Drop into the clough and turn
downstream for another surprisingly pleasant grassy walk, more
little falls and more room to manoeuvre than Linch Clough. The
stream will be crossed several times for convenience before arrival
at the confluence with the Westend river, an identical moorland
stream.** This is another super spot, imbuing a real feeling of being
hidden away, a true sanctuary. **Cross above the confluence and
continue south-west up the short, steep slope behind.** Part-way up,
look back over a bird's-eye view of the confluence to see Deep Grain
pointing at the Grinah Stones skyline, and the other clough pointing
directly at the Bleaklow Stones.

**Heading on, meanwhile, a trackless half-mile running south-west
skirting the knoll at 1755ft/535m leads onto the ridge descending
from Bleaklow, where a faint path will be found. Resume southerly
along this, through a dogged peaty saddle before rising to the white
painted OS column (S4298) at over 1640ft/500m on Westend Moor.**
The Kinder and Derwent edges still form great, long skylines.

A slowly improving path runs south, gradually declining and crossing to the edge above Alport Dale, a super moment. Here dubious terrain is exchanged for a charming 'edge' path. Enjoy increasingly good views into the meandering Alport river, contrasting with the sometimes harsh edges of the plantations, subject of controversial extraction plans: the hamlet also appears. **The path undulates along to a wall which then leads to the real bonus of the day, Alport Castles.**

This principal feature of WALK 19 also happens to be well placed to add a classic finale to our present ramble. This is a situation to savour, though lively young 'uns should not be let too near the edge. Pride of place goes to the remarkable Tower, which projects beneath us but high above Alport hamlet in the valley. The Tower has been isolated since an awesome landslip long ago, said to be the largest in Britain. It now stands as a proud sentinel and established landmark.

Leave from the wall terminus above the edge. A crumbling wall strikes across the moor, shadowed by the Alport-Derwent path. This quickly gains the head of Ditch Clough, absorbing a broader track and encountering grouse butts and a box cabin. Howden Reservoir appears ahead. **When the firmer track bears left remain on the grassy way into the head of the clough, then descend pleasantly past grouse butts.** Over to the left the Westend Valley is particularly well seen.

The grassy path drops down to a gate where the moor is finally left. Before doing so, pause to look left into the attractive Fagney Clough. **A hard track descends steeply through the trees, swinging right at the bottom to meet the road in the Derwent Valley as it negotiates a long, protruding arm of Howden Reservoir. Either turn left to enjoy a pleasant walk on grassy verges alongside the reservoir, or sit down and wait for the bus!**

Linch Clough

93

LOG OF THE WALKS

WALK	DATE	NOTES
1		
2		
3		
4		
5		
6		
7		
8		
9		
10		
11		
12		
13		
14		
15		
16		
17		
18		
19		
20		

INDEX

Principal features: walk number refers

THE PEAK DISTRICT

Explore on foot Britain's most popular National Park with a comprehensive set of 5 guidebooks. Each contains 20 walks.

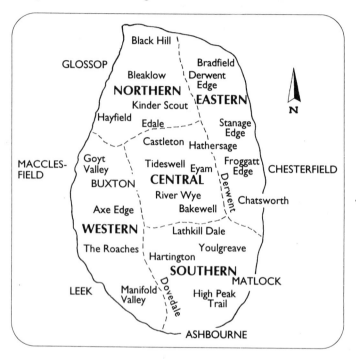

•**NORTHERN PEAK**   ISBN 1 870141 48 2
   Edale/Kinder Scout/Longdendale/Bleaklow/Hayfield/Mam Tor
•**EASTERN PEAK**   ISBN 1 870141 50 4
   Derwent Valley/Baslow/Eastern Edges/Chatsworth/Ladybower
•**CENTRAL PEAK**   ISBN 1 870141 51 2
   Bakewell/Wye Dale/Eyam/Monsal Dale/Tideswell/Miller's Dale
•**SOUTHERN PEAK**   ISBN 1 870141 52 0
   Dovedale/High Peak Trail/Lathkill Dale/Matlock/Tissington Trail
•**WESTERN PEAK**   ISBN 1 870141 54 7
   Buxton/The Roaches/Goyt Valley/Manifold Valley/Shutlingsloe